The Oldest Road   An Exploration of the Ridgeway

General map of the Route

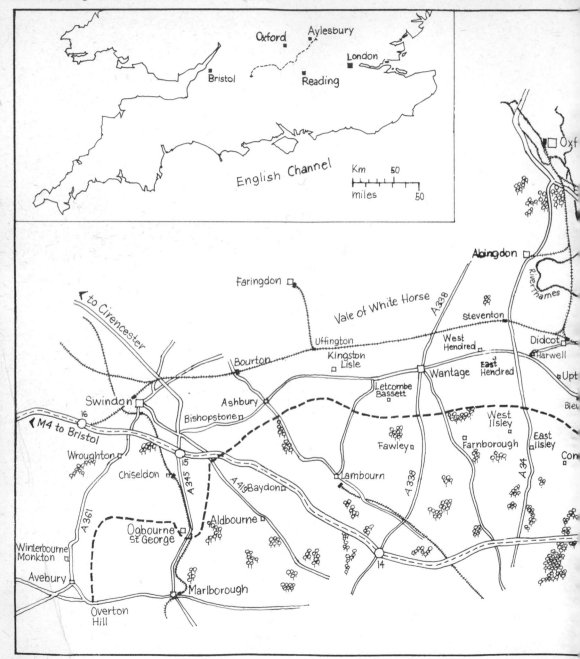

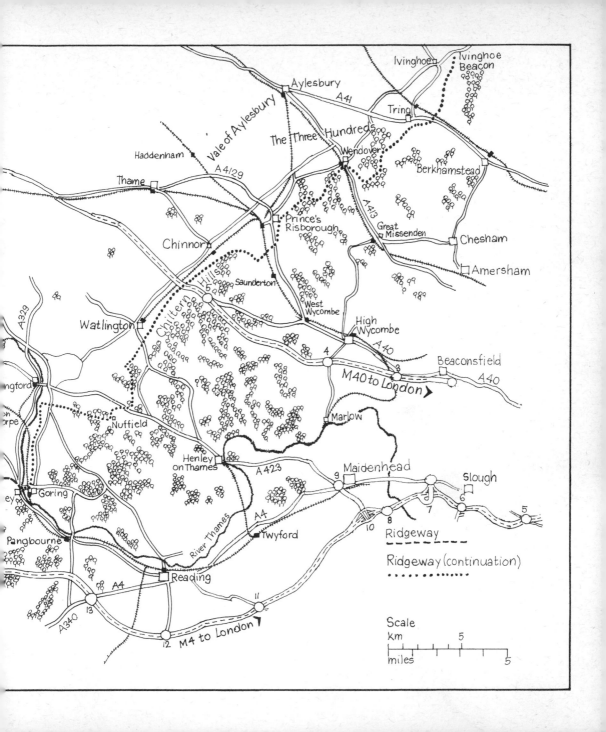

Ivinghoe
Ivinghoe Beacon
Aylesbury
A41
Tring
Vale of Aylesbury
The Three Hundreds
Haddenham
A4/29
Wendover
Berkhamstead
Thame
A413
Prince's Risborough
Great Missenden
Chesham
Chinnor
Saunderton
Amersham
Chiltern Hills
West Wycombe
Watlington
High Wycombe
A40
5
4
M40 to London
Beaconsfield
A40
A329
3
Nuffield
Marlow
ngford
Henley on Thames
A 423
Maidenhead
Slough
rpe
9
6
Goring
A4
7
5
ey
10
8
Pangbourne
River Thames
Twyford
Ridgeway — — —
Reading
Ridgeway (continuation) ••••••••
A4
11
13
A340
12   M4 to London

Scale
km   5
miles   5

The Photographs are for Dieter and Snowhill

The Oldest Road
An Exploration of the Ridgeway

Text: J. R. L. Anderson
Photography: Fay Godwin

Wildwood House London

First published 1975
Reprinted 1975
Text © 1975 by J.R.L. Anderson
Photographs © 1975 by Fay Godwin
Wildwood House Ltd
1 Wardour St, London W1V 3HE
Designed by Ken Garland and Associates
Maps drawn by Daria Gan

Typesetting by Red Lion Setters

Printed by Garden City Press Ltd
ISBN Hardback 0 7045 0167 8
ISBN Paperback 0 7045 0168 6
The maps are based upon the
Ordnance Survey Map with the
sanction of the Controller of H.M.
Stationery Office, Crown
Copyright reserved.

Contents

A Note about
this Book

Most roads have a beginning and an end, but the Ridgeway
has neither: what is left of it, and it is a remarkable stretch
for a road of such antiquity, starts nowhere and concludes in
time rather than in space. Since our conventions are finite,
and a book by convention must have a beginning and an end,
I have adopted for this study that portion of the ancient
Ridgeway which the Countryside Commission has marked
out as the Ridgeway Path. That begins tidily at Overton Hill,
near Avebury, and marches over some forty miles of the most
beautiful country in the world to the Thames. The
Commission, properly concerned with enabling people to
walk freely through as much countryside as possible, carries
its path across the Thames to follow the line of the Icknield
Way to Ivinghoe Beacon, near Tring. But the Commission's
public purposes are wider than mine, and for reasons that I
explain in the text my book is chiefly concerned with that
part of the Ridgeway that is south and west of the Thames:
the stretch, that is, that can still be identified clearly as —
that still *is* — the Ridgeway of antiquity. It must be
understood that this is only part of a road, the rest, save for
a few odd remnants here and there, having disappeared under
the plough and the bitumen of later roadmakers in the last
two thousand years of its long history.

We are so accustomed to react to our surroundings in their
practical state of length, breadth and thickness that we are
inclined to overlook their fourth dimension — time. But time
is as real a dimension as any other, often the dominant one,
and it is impossible to get the feel of the Ridgeway without a
constant awareness of its path through time as well as over

earth. In a sense, therefore, I have tried to make this a four-dimensional guide book. It will provide, I hope, all the practical information needed by anyone unfamiliar with the Wessex Downland to make a Ridgeway walk enjoyable and interesting: notes on physical characteristics run through the text, and a number of detailed suggestions about Ridgeway walking, and on getting to and from the Ridgeway itself, are grouped together in Chapter 9 which I have called 'Logistics'. All this, however, is only half the book, and I hope that the various signposts in time will be as useful to Ridgeway walkers as the rest. Time is a continuum — there is no 'now', for even as you say the word the present has already become the past. But within the infinite continuum of time it is both reasonable and convenient to mark off certain stretches as of particular or special interest. As I see it, there are three main periods in the Ridgeway's history: (1) The very early, prehistoric period, which saw the flowering of what I have called the Great Stone Culture (or civilization). (2) The misty centuries after the collapse of Roman power in Britain, during which the last remnants of Roman-British civilization rallied to fight a battle (which they ultimately lost) against the invading Saxons; in this period, the time of the semi-legendary King Arthur, the Ridgeway and its forts played, perhaps, a far more important part than has hitherto been assigned to them. (3) The better-documented (but still sadly neglected) period when history was curiously repeated, and King Alfred and the then-settled Saxons were fighting to hold Southern England against the invading Danes, or Vikings.

In the later two of these three periods the importance of the Ridgeway was primarily military. Even by Roman-British times the normal commerce of everyday life had ceased to have much use for a road running high above the spring-line as an ordinary means of communication. It served, as it does still, to give access to isolated farm-holdings on the high Downs, but travellers making their way from village to village followed a lower route, where they could be sure of water for themselves and their animals. For nine centuries after the Norman Conquest (in which the Ridgeway forts played no part) the Ridgeway countryside, for all its relative nearness to London, remained almost as isolated as the much remoter Highlands of Scotland: all main roads, and later, railways, ran north or south of it, and the Ridgeway itself was left to shepherds and the occasional traveller in search of solitude. One might, I think, add a fourth main period to the Ridgeway's history — the period in which we live, when it has found a whole new importance as a route of recreation. That period is just beginning, and it is up to contemporary society to see that the modern use of this most ancient of roads develops healthily. The chief danger to health comes from the motor car and motor cycle. Some are campaigning for their total prohibition on the Ridgeway, and anyone in love with the open spaces of the countryside must have much sympathy with this view. Reflection, however, cautions against it. Such a blanket prohibition would be alien to the whole history of the Ridgeway, as a road and not merely a footpath; moreover, down-grading it to a footpath would lay it open to the plough, which it has resisted for millennia; the path could be ploughed each year and although a right of way would remain it could not be at all the same thing as the existing ancient road. Tractors and other vehicles serving the high farms still use the Ridgeway, and they have a perfect right to do so. And those who are fit should not seek to deny access to the Ridgeway to those whose only hope of getting there is by car.

Nevertheless, motor traffic should be kept off the Ridgeway as far as possible. For much of its route the condition of the road itself is enough to discourage cars. There are a few convenient access-places, where cars can reasonably be parked but for the rest I should like to see notices requesting motorists not to drive on the Ridgeway at all. Such requests would deter all but the most selfish of drivers, and persistent selfishness would soon be punished by broken springs and other expensive damage. Such events as rallies and motor-cycle scrambles should certainly be prohibited, if necessary by an Act of Parliament. But the successors to the farm cart, and the man with a few months to live being driven a few hundred yards to let his dying eyes enjoy the view from Segsbury (an actual case, known to me), ought not to be interfered with.

In spite of the achievements of modern archaeology, any attempt to reconstruct the very distant past must involve much guesswork. Archaeology itself is not given to guesswork: archaeologists are trained to measure, to classify and to try to date physical objects. Beyond such limited conclusions as may properly be drawn from the age and position of their finds they are not supposed to indulge in fancy. They are concerned with what they *find*; they must not speculate too much on what they have not yet found, on what may lie hidden and never be found. The layman walking the Ridgeway and looking about him, gazing into time as well as into the sky, is not so restricted. I am indebted to the patient work of archaeologists for every physical fact that frames my observations, but my conclusions are very much my own. I differ, for example, from the canon of archaeological teaching in my interpretation of the age and original purpose of the Ridgeway's hill-forts. I do not say that I am right: all I say is that the standard interpretation seems to me to leave too much not only unexplained but inexplicable, and that my feeling — it can be no more — about these extraordinary structures is at least consistent with their location on the Ridgeway.

In my suggested Further Reading I have listed as faithfully as I can those works to which I have turned for help in making my own study. But it must not be thought that these authorities bear any responsibility at all for my observations. I differ from Mr John Morris *(The Age of Arthur)* in my suggested location of the Battle of Badon Hill, but that does not diminish my respect for his great learning, nor lessen my debt to his work. You cannot think for yourself unless you learn from others. So with all my authorities — I acknowledge my debt to them, but do not attempt to call on them to strengthen my own views.

Nomenclature has been a special problem. For thousands of years the Thames has been a boundary: in pre-Roman times between the Belgo-British tribes of the Catuvellauni and the

Atrebates, and, in its upper reaches, between the Catuvellauni and the non-Belgic Dobunni; later, between Wessex and Mercia; then between Anglo-Saxon England and the Danelaw; and until 1974 it was the county boundary between Oxfordshire and Berkshire. The reorganization of local government has now put North Berkshire, including most of the Berkshire Downs, into an enlarged Oxfordshire. It would be ludicrous to start calling them the Oxfordshire Downs: a name that has been in use for centuries cannot simply be unwritten at some planner's whim. Yet it is now incorrect to refer to the Berkshire Downs here, because they are not in Berkshire. I have, therefore, returned to what was probably an even older name, and called them the White Horse Downs. It is in keeping with history, and will, I hope, stick. At least no future fiddling with county boundaries can affect it.

This book is as much Fay Godwin's as mine, and I write for her as well as for myself in offering our exploration to the reader: a picture of an England that has survived the conquests and vicissitudes of ten thousand years, which will remain to enrich human imagination and delight human eyes for as long as this battered world contrives to avoid final catastrophe.

Where very many people have helped personally, and over many years, it is impossible fairly to acknowledge all, but I owe particular debts to Dr J.L. Mason and his colleagues of the Nature Conservancy Council, to Mr Geoffrey Wilson of the Countryside Commission (Department of the Environment), to my son Richard, who walked much of the Ridgeway with me, and to Helen, who did all the typing and much car-ferrying. For the rest, may I ask all my helpers known and unknown (for I have learned much from talking to strangers met by chance) to accept this collective acknowledgment of my thanks?

J.R.L. Anderson

1 The Road

A car is old at five years, pretty well finished at seven. A house lasts longer, but few houses are much use for living in after a century unless they have been patched and mended, constantly renewed. Old walls may stand for a long time, but roofs sag and fall in, and if masonry is left to weather on its own the green world of ivy, grass and trees soon wins. A house that has been cared for and lived in for three centuries is very old indeed. There are churches here and there in England where men and women have worshipped for nearly a thousand years, but they are rare and they stand as they do only because piety has kept watch against wind, rain and decay.

Most of us use little that has lasted for a hundred years. We may be proud to wear a father's watch or a mother's ring, but neither is likely to go back much over a century; when they do survive, such things are usually not in daily use but are kept in the vaults of a bank as valuable antiques. No human generation is quite self-sufficient; in spite of death duties and other laws against inheritance, we are bound to live to some extent on our fathers' capital, even if apparently they left us nothing. We use houses built by their hands, read books they wrote, enjoy gardens that they tilled. But mostly their work evaporates in three generations; houses fall down or are pulled down to make way for newer dwellings, gardens are built over, the books disappear into specialized libraries. Few great-grandfathers would recognize the surroundings of their great-grandchildren; hardly any would be other than puzzled by their way of life. This applies with special force in an era of swift technological change — men brought up to write with quill pens can scarcely be expected to understand typewriters — but equipment for human living has seldom outlasted three generations. Some old charters establishing the right of ancient towns to hold markets refer grandly to such markets as having been held from time beyond which the memory of man runneth not, but human memory in fact is neither particularly long nor particularly reliable. One hundred years is about the extreme limit of individual memory, and most memories cover no more than half a century. Reckoning three generations to a hundred years, the classical statistic, one may say that every fourth generation remakes the world.

Yet this is patently not true. We may not understand our grandfathers (or they us) but we are subject to the same needs, heirs to the same mortality. We may use different tools but we use them for the same jobs that men and women have always needed to perform: to provide food, clothing and shelter. Driving in a saloon car from centrally heated home to air-conditioned office, it is easy to forget that good or bad harvests still affect our lives, that we drink rainwater and need sunlight to ripen our food. Driving in a car . . . it is easier still to forget that the road we drive on is there because some forgotten forbear trod it out, that our houses, offices and shops are not where they are by chance, but because in every now-inhabited locality the soil, climate, the shelter of a hillside or river bank offered a livelihood and the chance of survival to some remote ancestor. Even if the road is a new one, built last year, it runs where it does because human feet once trod the way to a settlement, and then needed to get from one settlement to another.

Roads are the most enduring works of man. Partly, of course, they are works of nature, because man, with all other animals, seeks the easiest path to get where he wants to go, and the best route over or round hills, across rivers, or through jungles is determined by the structure of the land. Sheep-paths on a hillside follow the ledges of natural contours; the track to a water-hole runs where no rocks or great trees stand in the way. Once trodden by human feet, a natural path becomes a work

of man, each traveller marking the way for the next, sometimes departing from the most direct or obvious route to
avoid a muddy patch, or to keep out of sight of possible
enemies. Feet follow footsteps, and so a road is trodden into
history.

Roads may determine history. The prehistoric track from
Central Asia into India through the Khyber Pass, recognized
as a road at least since the Mauryan Empire in the fourth
century B.C., brought wave after wave of settlers and
conquerors into the Indian subcontinent. And long before
the Mauryans, the Khyber route, later the Grand Trunk Road
across India of the British Raj, determined the pattern of
human settlement in the Gangetic plain, and influenced the
development of human life in countless ways. As important
to England as the Khyber road has been to India is the
ancient track that follows the chalk Downs to provide routes
from the shores of the English and Bristol Channels to cross
the Thames at the Streatley-Goring Gap. That road, still called
the Ridgeway (though the Anglo-Saxon tongue is new
compared with the antiquity of the road), is still in daily use.
It has a fair claim to be considered the oldest road in Europe,
for men and women of the Old Stone Age walked it long
before Britain was an island, before the onset of the last Ice
Age. Swanscombe Woman, one of the earliest known members
of our own race of *homo sapiens*, left her skull in the gravel
of what is now the Thames Estuary (though the Thames was
then a tributary of the Rhine) about a quarter of a million
years ago. Her brothers doubtless wandered up the Thames
and took to the Ridgeway to hunt on the high ground of the
Downs — to get meat by killing an aurochs, the extinct
European wild ox which then roamed the English Downland.
Primitive chopping-stones or hand-axes from the Old Stone
Age have been found just off the Ridgeway near Marlborough.
Then the ice came, and *homo sapiens* went away. About
12,000 years ago, around 10000 B.C., the climate began
gradually to improve, England became habitable again, and
men and women of our own species began wandering back.
Again the Ridgeway on the high chalk offered a route across
Southern England clear of the difficulties and dangers of the

densely wooded, jungle-like valleys. Around 4000 B.C., the Ridgeway helped to shape one of the most decisive events in English history — settlement by an influx of new people who brought knowledge of how to live by farming and stock-rearing instead of depending on the chance of hunting.

These first Neolithic* farmers came by sea from Brittany or Spain, and they landed either on some western beach of the English Channel or on the shores of the Bristol Channel. They made their way inland by routes leading to the Ridgeway, and thence proceeded to clear settlements for themselves in the Wiltshire and Berkshire (since 1974, Oxfordshire) river valleys. They, and their successors, also spreading into England by the Ridgeway route, brought the beginnings of almost everything that makes up English national life. Alas, they did not bring writing, so much of what they did can be deduced only from what they left behind. But they left a great deal, including some of the most impressive tombs and the grandest stone monuments in the world.

A road runs through time as well as space. A signpost that tells you how many miles it is to Babylon could as fitly indicate how many years have passed since men first came that way from Babylon. The nursery rhyme embodies a practical sense of history:

> Can I get there by candlelight?
> Yes, and back again.

We can travel to the past only by the candlelight of imagination, but a road that leads directly from the past offers a number of physical signposts on the way. Did those early travellers on the Ridgeway come from Babylon? Not directly, but they came from the Eastern Mediterranean by

---

*The term 'Neolithic' is a bad one. It means 'New Stone' and is used to distinguish people with greater skills in making stone tools from the more primitive people of the 'Palaeolithic' ('Old Stone') Age. The vital discovery of the New Stone Age, however, was that man can feed himself by farming and stock-raising. 'Pastoralist' would be a better name, but 'Neolithic' is too entrenched in traditional archaeology to be changed.

way of Spain, and they brought knowledge of pastoral and agricultural skills discovered in the cradle of human civilization in the Near East. 'To Babylon 5,000 years', and 'To Crete 4,000 years' would not be inappropriate signposts on the Ridgeway.

What of the modern road? I have said that it is still in daily use, and it is, but not in the sense of the M4 motorway that

Uffington Castle

crosses it. The Ridgeway is not a metalled motor road, though it is used by the tractors and sometimes Land Rovers of the farmers whose fields lie on the high Downs. Because it is not a motor road the Ridgeway offers one of the finest walking routes in Europe — fifty miles or thereabouts of upland air from the northern scarp of the Vale of Pewsey along the great crescent of the Marlborough and White Horse Downs to the steep descent to Streatley, where there was once a ford (it must have been a fairly dangerous one) across the Thames to what is now Goring. You cross the river now by bridge and you can climb again into the Chilterns to follow the less ancient but still immeasurably old Icknield Way for another forty miles or so to Ivinghoe Beacon in Hertfordshire. In prehistoric times the chalk route ran on across the Dunstable Downs to Cambridgeshire and East Anglia to reach the sea near Hunstanton on The Wash. The Countryside Commission has marked a continuous track from Overton Hill, near Avebury, for some eighty-five miles to Ivinghoe Beacon, which it calls the Ridgeway Path and which is open to walkers for its whole length. Of course there are other stretches of footpath and ancient rights of way south and south-west of Avebury and north-east of Ivinghoe, but with the centuries the continuous track has disappeared, or has been incorporated in later roads.

The value of the Ridgeway Path is that it is a continuous route, signposted at doubtful places, where the walker can be sure of his right to be there — an admirable piece of public enterprise by the Commission. Strictly, I do not think that the route beyond the Thames can properly be called the Ridgeway: that is the oldest route of all, following the high Downs above the spring-line, where prehistoric man could travel in relatively open country, above the dangers that lurked in the thickly wooded lower slopes, and in the valleys. The Icknield Way, still a chalk route, runs more nearly on the spring-line, more convenient in giving travellers access to water; it came into use later, when there were fewer dangers from wolves and other wild animals in the woods. But it is still very old, and, oddly, this newer road has an older name than the more ancient route. The Ridgeway is just what its name implies in modern English, and it gets its name from the Anglo-Saxon '*hrycg*', meaning 'ridge'. Icknield is a name so old that it has no known root, and must embody some word from the forgotten tongue of unknown ancestors. Across the Thames the Icknield Way certainly became a continuation of the Ridgeway, providing a road across England from the south-western shores of the Channel to the North Sea. The Romans used stretches of the Icknield Way in their road system; they ignored the Ridgeway — it ran too high for them, and when they needed to move troops quickly they wanted to be sure of finding water on the route. It is loneliness and isolation that give the Ridgeway its special quality, and it is with the very ancient Ridgeway that this book is primarily concerned.

Why walk a prehistoric trackway that leads nowhere in particular, and, where it does give access of some sort to a village, goes a long way round to get there? First, perhaps, to find clean and lovely countryside well within a hundred miles of London, and nearer still to the great modern conurbations of Reading, Oxford and Swindon. Where the track runs on the bare, high Downs above Marlborough and Wantage you can go for miles without seeing a human habitation; it is unbelievably remote, and the sky reaches down to the land to make a horizon, something rarely found in our modern urban landscape. It is like being at sea — you sense that there is something different in the quality of your surroundings, and suddenly it strikes you that you can see a true horizon. It is infinitely refreshing, to both eyes and spirit.

Then there is the journey in time. You are no longer shackled within three generations — your own, your parents' and your children's. You walk in the footsteps of three hundred generations, seeing the same rounded hills, the same sky, tripping, it may be, over the same stone that stubbed a human toe ten thousand years ago. In our time-bound life it is good to move out of time, to feel that all the human politics and triumphs and disasters of ten thousand years — or twice ten thousand years — have left the road you walk unchanged. Often it must have seemed to your shadowy travelling companions that human life was in such a mess that it simply couldn't go on — yet the road runs on, and you, their two or three hundred times great-grandson, are there to tread it. This adds a useful perspective to time-foreshortened life.

Most travellers along the Ridgeway left no written record of their lives, but that is not to say they left no records. The road runs through a countryside rich with the relics of past peoples: graves of many different types and periods — long barrows apparently for group burial, round barrows for men, disc barrows for women; huge standing stones erected for purposes that now can only be guessed at, but erected with immense labour and impressive engineering skill; hill-fortresses and dykes; flint workings that were major industrial undertakings five thousand years ago; pots and beakers, loom weights, and bits and pieces that were once the everyday tools of living, now collected lovingly in museums. The ruts of tractors are superimposed on the ruts made by farm carts, and they on the hoofprints of pack-animals and the foot-prints of human porters. You can see fields terraced on the hillside three or perhaps four thousand years ago, side by side with great sweeps of modern ploughing made possible by the tractor. If you descend to a village you may see a man thatching a cottage roof, practising an art devised to keep out the rain long before Rome was heard of. You get a wonderfully *whole* perception of the persistence and continuity of life.

This book is primarily descriptive. My own forbears have lived around the Ridgeway for something like a thousand years (a trivial span in relation to the age of the road) which gives me a special interest in, and certainly a special love for, its countryside. But it gives me no special vision. I cannot see through your eyes, but I can sometimes suggest what other eyes should look for — the vision and the reward must be your own. Fay Godwin and I have produced this book in the hope of helping our fellow men and women to become aware of the marvellous national heritage we have in this most ancient of European roads.

Naturally, I hope that many readers of our book will want to

walk the Ridgeway for themselves. Please understand that it is a route to be travelled on foot, or perhaps on horseback — it is not for motor cars or motor cycles, and only doubtfully suitable for pedal cyclists. A highly acrobatic cyclist *might* manage some of its rougher stretches in dry weather, but some bits are very rough, and after rain more or less impassable for any wheeled vehicle other than a tractor. The Countryside Commission has signposted the way, but rightly it has done nothing to make the route anything other than it is — an ancient trackway trodden into history, steep as the hillsides themselves. The chalk turf dries quickly, but where the path is rutted it can be very muddy after rain. And wet chalk can be as slippery as a dance floor. You will need stout walking shoes or, better, a good pair of boots.

Remember that except where it occasionally descends steeply to climb again, the Ridgeway runs mostly above the spring-line. This means that no villages lie on it, and there are few habitations of any sort. You will need to carry food and water, and if you plan to spend some days on the route you will do best to travel completely equipped with provisions and a mountain tent. For those who may feel that their camping days are over, or who cannot spare the time for more than one day's outing, I have devised certain combinations of Ridgeway walking and meeting places by car to enable various stretches to be covered in turn. (See Chapter 9). This, of course, requires a car driven by someone else; if you drive yourself, you must leave the car somewhere, and walk back to it — pleasant enough, but inevitably limiting your range of walking. However, it is usually not all that difficult to find a friend or some member of the family who is prepared to do a bit of ferrying by car, and I shall suggest a number of things to see and places to visit to give the car-party a good day out.

Clothes, rucksacks and other pieces of equipment are so personal that advice is seldom welcome, but there are one or two practical points that may be overlooked unless you think of them beforehand. Remember that the Ridgeway climbs to nearly 300 metres (over 900 feet); the summits are exposed, and I reckon that you requre an extra pullover for the high Downs. The summits are usually windy too, and if you stop to rest or look about you, you soon grow chilly. If you walk in winter — and the exquisite clarity of light and air in a crisp December frost is a wonderful experience — bear in mind that roughly half the heat loss from the body comes from face and head, so that a woollen balaclava helps to keep one's whole body warm. Remember, too, that even when briskly walking on a winter's day your hands may get cold, so it is wise to have some gloves.

The Ridgeway runs through gentler country than that other great walk in Britain, the Pennine Way, but it is still high, exposed and lonely. You are never far from shelter and succour, but you are often some miles away, and mist can come down quickly. It is, therefore, sensible to have a compass. Apart from its value in an emergency a compass is always handy to orient yourself, and on any long walk you should never go without one.

I shall assume that any reader setting out to walk the Ridgeway will be familiar with the Ordnance Survey map. That trusted friend to most of us, the one-inch map (1 to 63,360), has been replaced by the new 1 to 50,000 series (2 centimetres to 1 kilometre, or approximately 1¼ inches to the mile). When I refer to the map it will be to the 1 to 50,000 sheet: map references are given in the margins. The maps provided in the book — scale 1:25,000 — precede the relevant chapters; the squares on these maps and the figures in the margins are the National Grid. You will find a general map of the Ridgeway Path on pp. ii-iii. If you have been brought up on the one-inch map (which first appeared in 1801) remember that places on the new map are slightly closer together than they seem to be. Although the contour lines on the new map are shown at intervals of fifty feet (because the sheet is a photographic enlargement of the old one-inch map) heights are now marked in metres. Tiresome as this is to anyone brought up to think in feet, I shall follow the new practice and give heights in metres (with the equivalent in feet in brackets, to comfort myself, if no one else).

Map A: Around Avebury

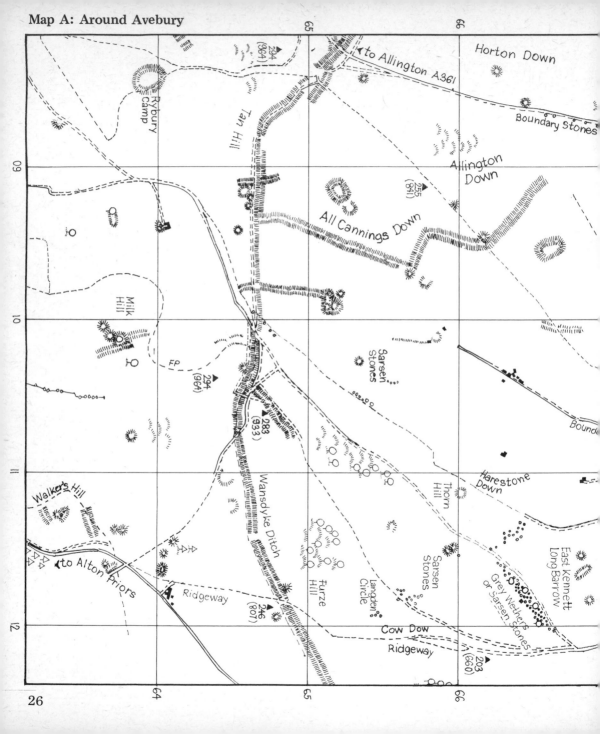

to Allington A361

Horton Down

Boundary Stones

Rybury Camp

Tan Hill

Allington Down

294 (964)

255 (841)

All Cannings Down

Milk Hill

FP

294 (964)

Sarsen Stones

283 (933)

Harestone Down

Thorn Hill

Bounde

Walker's Hill

Wansdyke Ditch

Sarsen Stones

Langdean Circle

Furze Hill

to Alton Priors

Ridgeway

Grey Wethers or Sarsen Stones

East Kennett Long Barrow

246 (807)

Cow Dow

Ridgeway

203 (660)

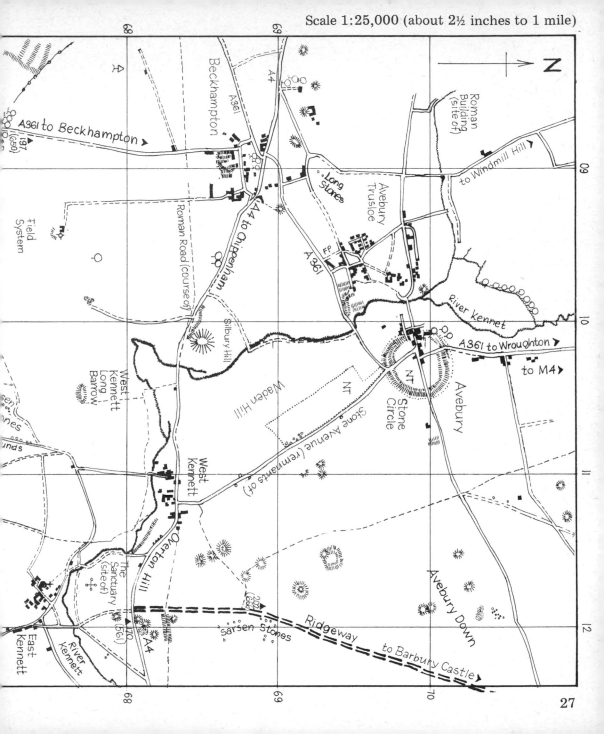

Scale 1:25,000 (about 2½ inches to 1 mile)

N

A361 to Beckhampton ▸

197 (650)

Field System

Beckhampton

A361

A4

Roman Road (course of)

A4 to Chippenham

Long Stones

Avebury Truslœ

FP

A361

Roman Building (site of)

to Windmill Hill ▸

River Kennet

A361 to Wroughton ▸

to M4 ▸

Silbury Hill

West Kennett Long Barrow

Waden Hill

NT

NT

Stone Circle

Avebury

Stone Avenue (remnants of)

West Kennett

Overton Hill

The Sanctuary (site of)

202 (663)

170 (561)

A4

Sarsen Stones

Ridgeway

Avebury Down

to Barbury Castle ▸

East Kennett

River Kennet

68

69

70

08

09

10

11

12

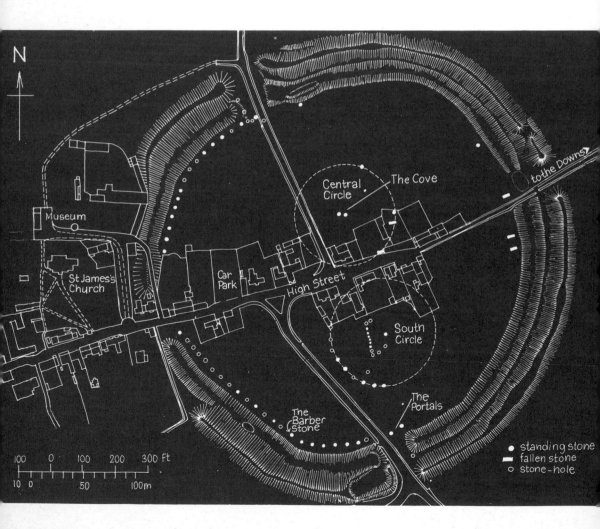

N

Museum

St James's
Church

Car
Park

High Street

Central
Circle

The Cove

South
Circle

The
Portals

to the Downs

The
Barber
Stone

● standing stone
━ fallen stone
○ stone-hole

100   0   100   200   300 Ft
10 0   50   100m

2   Metropolis of the Past

Avebury Ring

118681

The Countryside Commission starts its Ridgeway Path at Overton Hill, immediately to the north of the main road (A4), four and a quarter miles west of Marlborough. It is a good starting point for the modern walk, but the old Ridgeway had spurs running south-west to reach the Bristol Channel in the region of Bridgwater Bay (between Watchet and Weston-super-Mare) and south to join an ancient west-east track, roughly on the line of the modern A303, near Stonehenge. Other spurs ran on across Cranborne Chase and the Dorset Downs to reach the English Channel coast in the neighbourhood of Weymouth. The Ridgeway Path over the Marlborough and White Horse Downs to the Thames is the longest continuous stretch of the old route that still exists as an identifiable road, but stretches of its connecting tracks south-west and south can still be met with here and there. The Ridgeway in prehistory was a network of upland routes, in which the existing Ridgeway Path was, as it were, a stretch of the main road. It must be understood as such to realize its full importance in antiquity.

119679

That importance is apparent at Overton Hill. Just to the south of the modern main road, opposite the signpost indicating the start of the Ridgeway Path, is an enclosure marked on the map as 'The Sanctuary'. There is nothing much to see there now but concentric circles of concrete slabs marking the holes that once held great stones, and, earlier, wooden posts. A mile and a half to the north-east is the magnificent stone complex of Avebury, and linking the Avebury Great Circle to The Sanctuary is what was once a processional way between lines of huge stones, a few of which still stand. This

Avebury Ring (south-west
quadrant)

is called, rather inappropriately for a processional way bordered by stones not trees, 'Kennett Avenue', but romantic antiquarians were not always precise about nomenclature, and the name has stuck.

A day spent exploring around Avebury is a fitting preliminary to setting off along the Ridgeway. There is no problem here of car-ferrying, for you can stay the night in Avebury itself, or in Marlborough; leaving the car in Avebury, you can enjoy a splendid walking tour of what was once the metropolis not only of the Ridgeway countryside but also of prehistoric England and, possibly, of prehistoric Western Europe. Just as all roads were once said to lead to Rome, so the Ridgeway and its network of prehistoric routes led to Avebury a thousand years or more before Rome was built. But the Ridgeway is older than Avebury, so it was not trodden out to make a path there. Rather, Avebury and its associated groups of tombs and Great Stone monuments came into being where they are because the Ridgeway was there to serve them.

1069, 1070 The Great Stone Circle at Avebury is the greatest monument of its kind in the world, representing, with Stonehenge, some twenty miles to the south, a culminating peak of skill in the art of Megalithic (Great Stone) building, practised by prehistoric peoples in Brittany, Spain, some Mediterranean islands and elsewhere. The Avebury Circle consists of an immense circular bank towering above a ditch originally some fifty feet deep, and enclosing an area of about twenty-eight and a half acres. It is hard to visualize from figures alone: the sheer grandeur of the Avebury Circle is, perhaps, better expressed by saying that it encloses an area nearly four times the size of the whole area covered by the Houses of Parliament. In a ring round the crest of the bank about a hundred huge blocks of stone were erected, set in base holes specially constructed to receive them. The stones are enormous, some weighing at least forty tons. Many have disappeared, having been broken up to provide building stone for the neighbouring village of Avebury, but some remain standing, or have been re-erected in their original holes. Where the stones have gone but the stone-holes have been identified by archaeologists, concrete symbols have been placed to represent the missing stones. Inside the Great Circle there were once two and possibly three smaller circles of standing stones, parts of which can still be identified. Even after thousands of years of disuse and deliberate destruction, the Avebury Great Circle is impressive; in its full glory it must have been awe-inspiring.

Avebury is in many ways a more impressive work than Stonehenge, but for some reason, perhaps because of its enclosing Downs, it has never attracted as much popular attention. For centuries it was lost in local oblivion and was not written about until 1648, when John Aubrey (1626-97), the seventeenth-century antiquarian, came across the Great Circle one day while riding to hounds. He was so excited by the place that he declared it 'to exceed Stonehenge as a cathedral does a parish church'. It is a not invalid comparison, though it would be more meaningful to observe that the prehistoric metropolitan complex of Avebury exceeds Stonehenge as London, say, exceeds Salisbury.

There were more Great Stones standing in John Aubrey's day than there are now, for in the next century local builders discovered a technique for breaking up the huge monoliths by lighting bonfires of straw around them and then throwing cold water on the stones when they were hot. This provided admirable building blocks, cheaper and easier to get than quarried stone. Fortunately there was no large-scale property development in the region then, and sufficient of the monument survived for its restoration to be planned and largely carried out by the late Alexander Keiller, the last private owner of the property, who was a dedicated member of the Society of Antiquaries and financed archaeological work at Avebury up to the outbreak of the Second World War. In 1942 the site was acquired by the National Trust, and the monument is now safe from future property developers in the custody of the Ministry of Works (now incorporated in the Department of the Environment). It is a reflection of national indifference to so much of our national heritage that, had not this greatest of Megalithic monuments come into the

hands of a private individual who cared for antiquities, it might by now have been broken up completely.

The Great Circle and related complex of Megalithic building at Avebury and Overton appears to have achieved its peak of completed excellence between 2000 and 1600 B.C. The later parts of the work are attributed to a people known (from the characteristic shape of the pottery they left behind them) as the Beaker People. They came originally from Spain, and there seem to have been several waves of Beaker immigration, some by sea directly to the Channel coast, and some by groups of the same race who had made their way across France to the Low Countries, across the North Sea to the Thames estuary, and thence up-river. The western groups followed the Ridgeway inland from the coast, while their north-eastern cousins coming up the Thames met the route at its other end, at Streatley. Avebury doubtless served as a tribal meeting place, and the immense labour of Megalithic building there is perhaps explained by the need to have a tribal centre as a place of pilgrimage, and a setting for national — or international — religious ceremonies. Archaeological evidence has shown that pilgrims came from at least as far away as the Rhineland, and they may have come also from Spain and Brittany, where there were also Great Stone Cultures of the same, or a related, people.

These Beaker immigrants appear to have been a tough, intelligent people, and they seem fairly quickly to have established themselves as a ruling class over the Neolithic farming community already living in the area. Technologically they were undoubtedly superior to the resident population, for they brought with them some knowledge of metal working, and were the forerunners of the Bronze Age in Britain. A Bronze Age culture gave them obvious advantages over a people still living in the Stone Age, and they seem, too, to have had considerable enterprise as merchants. The Neolithic farmers of Wessex were, on the whole, a prosperous lot, and the Beaker immigrants seem to have done well out of selling them bronze vases and metal trinkets, among them occasional ornaments of gold. Their possession of such

The Barber Stone

precious goods to sell no doubt gave them prestige, and helped them to gain dominion over the local populace. There are no metal ores in the chalk Downlands of the Ridgeway countryside, but the Downs do offer one raw material that had been of great value earlier — flint of high quality for flaking into sharp blades for Stone Age tools. Routes for the flint trade were long established on the Ridgeway when the Beaker immigrants came, and it seems likely that they took

Some of the stones in the
Circle at Avebury; note the
Cove *below* and Portals *right*

over much of this trade, which continued to be important for
centuries after the first rare bronze tools began to make their
appearance. Beaker merchants got metal ores from Wales,
Cornwall and Ireland, making adventurous journeys in pursuit
of trade. There was no money in England then, and people
were still a thousand years or more away from the iron bars
that began to serve as currency in the much later Iron Age.
All trade was by barter — so many flints, or a bronze knife
in return for grain, hides or slaves. Like successful merchants i
many other periods of human history the Beaker traders
probably soon had many of the local farmers in their debt,
which no doubt helped when they wanted labour to work on
the building of the Great Stone circles.

Stone-moving and stone-raising was made easier for the
Beaker architects and overseers by the fact that there was

already a Megalithic tradition in the region. Far older than the Stone circles at Avebury are some of the barrow-tombs nearby, and these, too, required the moving and erection of great stones for their construction. Some of the Neolithic farmers brought a Great Stone Culture with them, originating some think, from an ancestral homeland in Crete. Migrating into England by the Ridgeway route they found a magnificent supply of huge boulders in the sarsen stones that are common

in some areas of the Wiltshire Downs. These stones have always had a certain mystery about them, for they do not belong in chalk country. They are the remnants of a sandstone cap that once covered parts of the area; broken up by millennia of weathering and glaciation, the remaining boulders were left scattered about the Downs as the last Ice Age receded. To medieval eyes they appeared to have come by magic, and the name 'sarsen' derives from 'Saracen', the Saracens being regarded as powerful magicians in legends and tall stories brought back from the Crusades. They sometimes still seem magical, and although archaeologists and engineers have worked out ways by which stones weighing many tons could have been transported on tree-trunk rollers and erected with the aid of wooden levers and rawhide ropes, anyone who did not actually take part in the work may well have felt that they were placed there by magic, to stand

guard over tombs, or to sanctify stone circles. The earlier
Neolithic people — or their priests and chieftains, who
understood the art of moving boulders — used sarsens to
inspire awe for the tombs of their important dead, and the
Beaker newcomers, with their superior skills, worked on the
old tradition to achieve new marvels of Megalithic building.

Freshly broken sarsen has something of the honey-coloured
warmth of Cotswold stone, but it weathers to a smooth,
dark surface that may be anything from the deepest purple to
a reddish grey, sometimes an almost iridescent mingling of
every shade from indigo to pink. The texture is oddly
exciting, thrilling to the fingertips like a small electric shock.
One can, and, to get the sense of them properly, one should,
walk up and touch these stones: unlike so many other
antiquities, they will not suffer from the touch of many hands.

The stones for the Great Circle at Avebury itself probably
came from Overton Down and the adjoining Fyfield Down,
two to three miles to the east, where there is a peculiarly
rich outcrop of sarsens. This is quite near — but think of
moving a forty-ton block of stone over a few yards, let alone
two miles, of rough country! Fyfield Down also provided the
sarsens for Stonehenge, a distance of over twenty miles. Great
skill must have gone into the selection of each stone. Before
being erected they were roughly shaped into the 'lozenges' or
'pillars' required, but the purpose of such shaping seems to
have been mainly to enhance the natural shape of the stone,
rather than to alter it. Long searches and careful measuring
were required to find precisely the right stone for each
location.

Please, may any lingering ideas that the Druids had anything
to do with Stonehenge or the Avebury Circles be finally and
totally abandoned? These monuments were old a thousand
years before Druids were heard of in Britain. The Druids
served Teutonic-Celtic cults and practised their rites in the
groves of dark forests. They came to England with the
invasion of Belgic tribes in the last few centuries B.C., and
could have had nothing whatever to do with the Great Stones.

Avebury: stone in south-east
quadrant of Great Circle.
Opposite Detail of the same
stone

Furthermore, to relate Druidism to these Great Stone monuments is culturally absurd. We do not know what religious rites were practised at Stonehenge and Avebury, but whatever they were they belonged to a religion of light and air, not to the dark mysteries of forests. Peopling these monuments with Druids is a piece of nineteenth-century romanticism by people with no feeling for the spirit of a place and no knowledge of the archaeological facts.

Graves have been found at the foot of some of the Avebury stones, but there is nothing to suggest that these are anything more than what they appear to be — burials in a sacred place, from precisely the same motive as that which secured the burial of distinguished men in later ages in Westminster Abbey and St Paul's. The skeleton of one man found underneath a fallen stone suggests that any modern inquest would return a verdict of 'Accidental Death'. He was neither

Neolithic peasant nor Beaker overlord, but a man of the fourteenth century, apparently a travelling barber-surgeon; he had with him an early type of lancet, a pair of scissors, and some coins of the reign of Edward I (1239-1307). His neck was broken and his leg was trapped as the boulder fell. The circumstances suggest that he was lending a hand in an attempt to shift the stone, perhaps for breaking up as building stone, when it fell and crushed him. He was killed outright, and the villagers, or whoever was with him, could not move him, so they covered him with earth and he was buried where he fell. His scissors (now in the Avebury Museum) are the earliest pair of scissors to come to light in England.

There is nothing to indicate that any cult of human sacrifice was ever associated with the Great Stone Culture of the Ridgeway countryside. The grim name of the Slaughter Stone at Stonehenge has no archaeological justification: it is a morbid antiquarian fancy. 'There is no evidence at all for supposing that human sacrifice was practised at Stonehenge at any time during its long history,' writes Professor R.J.C. Atkinson in his *Guide to Stonehenge and Avebury.* *

After this brief introduction it is time to start exploring. A car can be left conveniently in the car park at Avebury, and the first thing is to climb the embankment of the Great Circle and walk round it. It is somewhat disconcerting to discover that the earthwork is bisected by the modern road from Devizes to Swindon (A361), but less so than it seems, for the circle was designed with entrances at each cardinal point, and it was divided into quadrants by a crossing of what were probably processional routes. The modern road makes an awkward right-angled turn to enter the Circle from the south, originally the entrance for the processional way (Kennett Avenue) leading to The Sanctuary at Overton Hill. This entrance is additionally complicated by serving also the modern road to Marlborough (via Overton Hill) which runs beside the old processional way. The Devizes-Swindon road runs out from the north. The western entrance gives directly

Avebury: the Avenue

*H.M. Stationery Office, London, 1959, revised 1971

43

to the village that grew up in the place, using the stones as material for many of its own buildings. The eastern entrance (it is actually slightly north of east) still has a green road or footpath that runs towards the Downs to join the Ridgeway about a mile and a half away. On the one-inch Ordnance Survey map this road is marked as the *'herepath'*, a term used by the early Anglo-Saxon settlers to distinguish a green road from a Roman road, which they called a *'straet'*. The term *'herepath'* is a general one, there seems no particular reason for its use here, and the name has been dropped from the new 1:50,000 map, though the path connecting with the Ridgeway is, of course, marked.

What does one feel across the centuries — millennia, rather — on perambulating a monument whose purpose is unknown, and whose builders are unnamed (save in archaeological terms), the hopes and fears of those it served long forgotten? The place holds strongly what the Latin tongue called *'religio loci'*, a term that sounds wooden in the English 'spirit of a place'. This is because we have lost practically all formal sense of standing anywhere on hallowed ground — we visit cathedrals or battlefields mostly as tourists, seldom as pilgrims. But a sense of awe, unconscious or half-conscious perhaps, persists in modern man and I think most people will feel it here, even if they do not recognize what they are feeling. The great bank, the stones, the setting still have meaning, although only imagination can suggest what their meaning is. It is not quite the same meaning as in a great temple of some alien faith: there the sense is clear, you are visiting a monument erected to the glory of God, maybe not your own God, but a Godhead you accept as manifesting other men's piety — you feel that mixture common to mankind of pride in being human and despair at the littleness of man. You get something of the same feeling but there's more to it than that, for these Great Stone monuments are not wholly alien, we cannot know what faith inspired them, but it was a faith that inspired men and women living and working in our own country, who are among our own remote ancestors.

Reflecting on such thoughts as you will, I suggest that you

The Avenue: three views of the same stone

103697   leave the Great Circle by the southern entrance, and take the processional way (it runs a little east of south) to Overton Hill. This is a magnificent route (marked as 'Stone Avenue' on the map) wide and straight, still offering a sense of grandeur even though only a few of its original two hundred or so pairs of Great Stones are standing. the stones are roughly, but seemingly deliberately, shaped in two forms: one a straight, square pillar, the other a broad diamond or lozenge,

mounted at one point of the diamond. They are weathered and roughened now, but there can be no doubt of the original intention to have pairs of stones in these two shapes. Those who are inclined to see phalluses and wombs in everything conclude at once that the tall, straight stones are male, the diamond-shapes female. The pattern seems to have been followed for the stones of the Great Circle, too, and the interpretation is not necessarily far-fetched. As distinguished (and critical) an archaeologist as Jacquetta Hawkes writes of the contrasting shapes: 'Even the most austere archaeologists are prepared to concede that they may well stand for females and males, and represent a fertility cult among the rites celebrated at Avebury.'* It may be so; but the shaped stones may equally represent the sun and moon, or clear and clouded sky. We do not, and cannot ever, know. This is another case of meaning without interpretation, or rather of meaning, the interpretation of which must be left to imagination.

The Wansdyke

119679   Of the so-called Sanctuary (the name is another modern one) at Overton I have already written briefly. There is nothing now to see except concrete stumps marking stone or post-holes, and it is not worth spending much time here. Peter Fowler, in his Archaeology of Wessex, has an interesting drawing suggesting how the place may have looked around 1600 B.C. It shows a circular timber structure, roofed with thatch, surrounded by an outer circle of Great Stones, with an entrance from the processional way (Kennett Avenue). Certainly there does seem to have been a timber building here, for traces of rotted wood have been found in the post-holes, but there is no indication that the place was ever inhabited in any ordinary sense. It is reasonable to think that priests and acolytes or virgins serving the stone temples needed somewhere to keep robes and sacred emblems, and the wooden structure may have been a sort of vestry. This structure, though, would have been large for a vestry, and Professor Atkinson in his guide suggests that the early

*Jacquetta Hawkes, *A Guide to the Prehistoric and Roman Monuments in England and Wales* (Chatto and Windus, London, 1951, revised 1973).

A coombe near the Wansdyke

East Kennett Long Barrow

Small stone circle at Thorn Hill

Neolithic settlers may have had a wooden temple there, the sacred site being taken over and embellished with Great Stones by the later Beaker people. This is in keeping with human experience elsewhere. At Garford, in the Vale of the White Horse, a Roman temple was built on the site of what seems to have been an Iron Age shrine, and the place was later used for Anglo-Saxon burials. The spirit of a place once held sacred long persists.

At Overton Hill Sanctuary you are on the Ridgeway, and although the signposted Ridgeway Path across the A4 runs north, it is worth going south past the little village of East Kennett at least as far as the great earthwork known as the Wansdyke, a walk of roughly two miles. It is magical country of rolling hills, with several rising to near 300 metres (over 900 feet), forming the huge northern escarpment of the Vale of Pewsey. It is mostly bare, and if you see a herd of cows on a skyline they look like a frieze. There are a few coppices and occasional clumps of trees, planted as windbreaks or sometimes to mark a barrow, but one's whole impression is of space and sky and the bareness of hill-turf.

The huge ditch of the Wansdyke is finely preserved here for some six or seven miles. It runs roughly east to west, tending a little north at the western end. Originally, it ran for some fifty miles from the neighbourhood of Inkpen, at the point where the modern counties of Berkshire, Hampshire and Wiltshire meet, to the Bristol Channel somewhere near Portishead. Much of it has disappeared under fifteen hundred years of ploughing, but on the high Downs here you can see a magnificent stretch of it almost as it was made. The ditch has shallowed a bit with the passage of fifteen centuries, and the embankment, once a towering earth battlement, has rounded with weathering, but you can see what a formidable defence it was. A defence against whom? It is clearly against attack from the north, for it is dug with the ditch to the north of the great embankment; manned by determined men it would have been a fearful obstacle to scale. In its final form at any rate it is post-Roman, for farther west stretches of the embankment are to be found built on top of a Roman road, but when and by whom it was built is unknown. Archaeologists think that it dates from some time in the fifth century, when Roman power had collapsed and the surviving Roman-British population was struggling to resist invading Saxons. The Saxons undoubtedly held the Upper Thames north of the Ridgeway, and Jacquetta Hawkes has a theory that the Wansdyke was constructed by Ambrosius Aurelianus, the last of the professional Roman-British generals, to hold the south and south-west against the Saxons. Ambrosius is believed to have been a kinsman, possibly an uncle, of the legendary King Arthur, and there seems no doubt that he, perhaps with Arthur as his lieutenant, rallied the Britons and, around the year 500 (some date it more precisely at 493) won a decisive victory over the Saxons at a place called *Mons Badonicus* (Badon Hill).

Bede, in the first great work of English history (written between about A.D. 709 and 731) describes the sequence of events thus:

When the victorious invaders [the Saxons] had scattered and destroyed the native peoples . . . the Britons slowly began to take heart and recover their strength, emerging from the dens where they had hidden themselves, and joining in prayer that God might help them to avoid complete extermination. Their leader at this time was Ambrosius Aurelianus, a man of good character, and the sole survivor of Roman race from the catastrophe. Among the slain had been his own parents, who were of royal birth and title. Under his leadership the Britons took up arms, challenged their conquerors to battle, and with God's help inflicted a defeat on them. Thenceforward victory swung first to one side and then to the other until the battle of Badon Hill, when the Britons made a considerable slaughter of the invaders. *

Mons Badonicus has never been identified, though it must have been somewhere near the northern end of the Ridgeway. Jacquetta Hawkes's theory seems to me probable. I shall

*Bede, *A History of the English Church and People,* translated by Leo Sherley-Price (Penguin, Harmondsworth, 1955, revised 1968).

discuss it, and the possible location of Badon Hill, in more detail when we come to consider the hill-forts along the northern stretches of the Ridgeway. The Saxons themselves, at least in their pagan period, considered the Wansdyke to have been built by magic. The name we have for it is Saxon, and it means 'Woden's Dyke', implying a dyke constructed by Woden's supernatural powers.

In the two miles from Overton Hill to the Wansdyke we have moved through some two and a half thousand years, from around 2000 B.C. to A.D. 500 — a longer span of time than that which separates the present day from Julius Caesar's landing in Britain in 55 B.C. This is the endless fascination of the Ridgeway — our footprints merge with those of shadowy Neolithic peasants, rich Beaker merchants, the soldiers of Ambrosius and their Saxon enemies, later Saxon settlers, Normans, and of every English generation since the fusion of many races that produced the English people of the twentieth century. We must now go back again in time to our earlier period in the third millennium B.C.

The few square miles of Downland enclosed between the Ridgeway south of East Kennett, the Wansdyke and the Devizes road (A361) that crosses the Wansdyke some five miles west of the Ridgeway hold memorials of man from the most remote and shadowy past up to the present. The map is peppered with the symbols and the Gothic lettering that the Ordnance Survey uses to indicate antiquities, long barrows, earthworks, standing stones and what it calls 'tumuli', mostly round barrows covering the graves of prehistoric man, or even, it may be, of someone's beloved horse of a much later century. This is very much horse country, and on the smooth turf of the Downs are the training gallops of modern racehorses, superb and highly-bred, among the most beautiful animals on earth. The tractor has taken over from the work-horse, but many people nowadays accept the double-bass throb of the tractor as one of the distinctive sounds of the countryside. I don't wholly; tractor-sound is not obtrusive as long as it is distant, but I regret the presence of tractors in a world that belongs to lark-song and

Overleaf Silbury Hill

silence — that *living* silence of rounded hills under the great
bowl of the sky. But the tractor belongs to man as much as
the Great Stones. I daresay inhabitants of the Downland five
or six thousand years ago regretted the fidgeting of
newcomers who wanted to move Great Stones about the
place. Neither they nor I can halt change; the marvel here is
the continuity of life in spite of change.

Going west along the Wansdyke from where the Ridgeway
meets it, a walk of just over two miles brings you to a footpath leading over Allington Down back towards Overton Hill.
The path leaves the Wansdyke at map reference 083651, but
there are two tracks leaving the Wansdyke just about here.
One, going almost due north, leads to Beckhampton; you
want the track going north-east. After about two miles it
turns almost due east for Overton, and about a quarter of a
mile to the west of the turn is another of the famous
antiquities of Europe, the West Kennett Long Barrow. North-
west of the Long Barrow, on the north side of the main road
(A4) is yet another, the extraordinary artificial hill called
Silbury Hill.

You have now a choice of routes and actions, depending on
the time you have in hand, the weather, and your feeling for
just strolling on the Downs. You can make your way by
104677   footpaths to the West Kennett Long Barrow, the largest
monument of its kind in Britain; thence back to the main
102685   road (A4) near Silbury Hill, and after crossing the road you
can walk from Silbury Hill to Avebury (about a mile) across
country. Or you can go back to the car before visiting the
Long Barrow and Silbury, and drive round to them. Silbury
is right by the main road (A4) and across the road, nearly
opposite the hill, there is a signposted footpath to the West
Kennett Long Barrow (about half a mile). If you are
walking near the foot of Silbury Hill be cautious of the ditch
that surrounds it. Much of the ditch looks shallow and almost
filled in, but it floods readily, and even in apparently dry
weather it can be unpleasantly boggy.

Silbury Hill has come down to us as the most massive folly in

Europe. It is simply a man-made hill with a flat top, of the sort children make with buckets of sand. But Silbury is of gigantic size — it stands 40 metres (130 feet) high, and covers five and a half acres. It is surrounded by a ditch, from which the earth to build it came. This ditch was originally 38 metres (125 feet) wide and 9 metres (30 feet) deep. It can still be seen, but it has been much flooded over the centuries and it is now largely filled in with mud. The people who made this enormous hill had nothing but antler-picks, bits of wood and the shoulder-blades of oxen to use as shovels, and baskets to move earth in. It has been estimated that the work would have taken five hundred men at least ten years (other estimates make it seven hundred men). All one can say is that the work of making the hill must have taken a large labour force a very long time. Archaeologists date the hill to about 2100 B.C., rather before the flowering of the Great Stone Culture, though some of the barrows using Great Stones in their construction are earlier than 2100 B.C. The work of digging and earth-moving to build Silbury is similar, though on a larger scale, to that of making the ditch and embankment for the Avebury Stone Circle, or of covering a big barrow. The scale of the work at Silbury, however, required refinements of civil engineering technique not found elsewhere: to prevent landslips the earth-body of the hill is strengthened by interior walls of chalk, and the side-wall of the ditch against the base of the hill was also strengthened with rammed chalk.

Various expeditions from the eighteenth century onwards have tunnelled into the hill without finding anything to explain its purpose. If it covers a ceremonial grave, no tomb has yet (1974) been found. The flat top, with a sort of terrace round it near the summit, rather suggests that the whole edifice may have been planned as the plinth of a Great Stone circle, but the date (if it is anywhere near right) seems too early for a Great Stone setting of such sophistication; and there is nothing to indicate that any attempt was ever made to erect stones on it. Perhaps the conception was simply too ambitious, a splendid failure like Brunel's *Great Eastern*, a ship so far in advance of any previously built that the services needed to sustain such a great vessel just did not exist.

West Kennett Long Barrow
Overleaf

If Silbury was in some sense a failure, as a piece of civil engineering it was a brilliant success. It has kept its shape for four thousand years, a marvellous record for an earthwork without masonry. The unknown engineer who built it can properly be called a genius.

Across the busy modern road a pleasant footpath leads to the West Kennett Long Barrow, a little under half a mile from

104677

Above and left West Kennett
Long Barrow (entrance)
Overleaf Interior

the road. This huge tomb, covered by a coffin-shaped mound
330 feet long and 80 feet across at its widest (eastern) end, is
very old indeed, being dated at about 2500 B.C., or even
rather earlier. It was partly excavated in 1859, when a burial-
chamber containing six burials was found. A much more
detailed investigation was carried out a century later (1955-6)
by Professor Stuart Piggott and Professor R.J.C. Atkinson.
They found that the barrow covered not one burial-chamber
but five, one at the western end and two opening from each
side of a roofed drystone passage. The pillars and capstones
were sarsens common to the neighbourhood, but some of the
walling stones were formations that do not occur locally and
seem to have been brought from Calne, six miles away, and
Frome, twenty miles away. There were skeletons, considerably
damaged, apparently by prehistoric tomb-robbers, of at least
forty-six people, men, women, children and some young
babies. Pottery found among the grave-goods buried with the

people ranged in date from 2500 B.C. or earlier to distinctive work of the Beaker period around 1600 B.C. The tomb was, therefore, in use for something like a thousand years, perhaps as the mausoleum of a dynasty, or (more likely) of successive ruling families.

The entrance to the tomb is at the eastern end, with an impressive forecourt flanked by tall sarsen pillars. Some of the stones inside have still-identifiable 'sharpening' marks — polished patches where, it is thought, stone tools used in the work were sharpened.

At some time, presumably after about 1600 B.C., the entrance to the tomb was formally blocked by a row of great sarsens, one huge boulder standing twelve feet high. Whether it was decided that the tomb was full, or whether burial practice changed, no one can say. From the care that was taken to block the tomb with ceremonial Great Stones it would seem that it remained a sacred place after burials ceased, perhaps an object of pilgrimage, with religious ceremonies of some sort continuing to be held there. The Ministry of Works (Department of the Environment) has carefully restored the barrow after excavation, and re-erected stones that had slipped or fallen over the centuries. Archaeological finds from the excavation can be seen in the Museum of the Wiltshire Archaeological and Natural History Society in Devizes.

The river-name 'Kennett' shared by the two small villages that lie north and south of the stream, is of great antiquity. The Roman Marlborough (about a mile to the east of the present town) was called 'Cuneito', which is clearly 'Kennett' in a Latin form. But Cuneito is not a Latin word, and when they laid out a small town on the bank of the river Kennet the Romans simply used the existing name for the place. Where does it come from? Some scholars have sought to identify the root 'Ken-' with the Welsh 'Cyn-' which can mean 'high', or in some contexts 'royal'. Yet 'Kennett' is far older than the Saxons, and cannot possibly derive from a Saxon word. Did the Saxons pick it up, via the Romans, from the ancient tongue of the folk who lived in the Ridgeway countryside, to whom the Great Stones of Avebury and the huge monuments of Silbury Hill and the West Kennett Long Barrow must have been awe-inspiring and royal indeed? It is certainly possible that this metropolis of Great Stone Culture was known as 'the royal place', and that the very ancient name survives in 'Kennett'.*

The West Kennett Long Barrow belongs to a type of passage grave also found in various parts of North-west Europe, France, Spain and Portugal, and in the British Isles in the Cotswolds, Wales, Scotland and Ireland. The wide spread of this early Megalithic culture emphasizes the importance of the metropolitan complex here — conceivably some priestly dynasty interred in the West Kennett Long Barrow was respected from the Irish Sea to the Mediterranean. The West Kennett Barrow is particularly interesting by reason of its size, and also because of its comparatively early date, reasonably attested by the pottery found there, which can be related to known archaeological sequences. It used to be thought that most of the passage graves in Europe belonged to a period around 2000 B.C. which made the substantial edifice at West Kennett seem peculiarly early. However, recent work in carbon-dating (based on the known rate of decay of radio-active carbon present in all organic matter but not renewed after death) has suggested that many formerly accepted dates must be set back — i.e. that some structures are considerably older than used to be thought. Two passage graves in Brittany have been dated to between 3500 and 3000 B.C.,† which puts the Neolithic builders of the West Kennett Long Barrow, who are thought to have come to South-Western England from Brittany or Spain, in a reasonably chronological relationship with their Continental cousins and forbears.

Carbon-dating is an invaluable archaeological tool, but it can

*'Kent' (the county), which at first sight seems rather similar to 'Kennett' was known to the Romans as *'Cantium'* (not the root *'Cun-'* as in *'Cuneito'*) and probably derives from a Celtic word meaning 'coast-land'.
†Professor Glyn Daniel, *The Megalith Builders of Western Europe,* (Hutchinson, London, 1958, new edition Penguin, Harmondsworth, 1962).

be used only for organic matter — bones, wood, leather, etc. The still-newer technique of thermo-luminescent dating, which can be applied to pottery, may bring about considerable revision of what now seem to have been probable dates in antiquity. But a word of caution is necessary about all dating techniques, however scientifically accurate they may be — in order to be dated, objects have first to be found. And they must have some probable contemporary relationship with whatever one is trying to date from them. If a museum, say, containing many objects of the second millennium B.C., were to be destroyed by fire, it would not be reasonable to say from an examination of the rubble that the building must have been three to four thousand years old. If a piece of pottery that can be dated to 2500 B.C., comes to light in some very ancient settlement or structure, it can be assumed that it goes back at least to 2500 B.C: it cannot safely be assumed that the place is not considerably older. Bits of pottery more ancient still may be found later, or they may be lying in the ground somewhere and never found. In thinking about the distant past it is often wiser to think in rather general terms of centuries and millennia than to attempt more precise dates. A century is long for one lifetime, but an almost insignificant part of four thousand years.

There is much of more modern interest to see around Avebury: the charming village itself, an exceptionally well-arranged museum, a beautiful Norman church incorporating pieces of earlier Saxon workmanship, and a fine Elizabethian manor house with a dovecot and an enchanting garden. One cannot attempt to see everything in one day. It is a good idea to visit the museum before setting off to walk on the Ridgeway, because the exhibits there will help to give meaning to much that you will see as you walk, but whether you spend two or three days around Avebury at a stretch, or pay the place several visits is a matter of choice. A day in Avebury itself will make a pleasant way of passing the time for a car-party waiting to collect a walking party from an exploration of the Ridgeway.

There is a further diversion from Avebury that is worth

The Devil's Den

152697
(Map B)

157688
(Map B)

making before starting to walk the Ridgeway proper, and that is to a curious dolmen called 'The Devil's Den' at Clatford Bottom, on the eastern edge of Fyfield Down. It means going back about three and a half miles towards Marlborough, but this is along the main road (A4), and the dolmen is easily reached by a walk of just under a mile from the main road.

From Avebury go back towards Marlborough until just beyond Fyfield village. The track you want is northgoing (that is, on the left-hand side of the road going towards Marlborough) about half a mile out of Fyfield. The only difficulty here is in finding the right track, because there are two northgoing paths within a couple of hundred yards of each other. You need the more westerly of the two, the first you come to after Fyfield. This offers a pleasant open walk towards the Downs — the more easterly track is overgrown and confined between thick hedges. After half a mile or so along the track you come to a big barn: the dolmen is about half a mile farther on, standing solitary in a wide expanse of what is now arable land. It is a strange trilithic monument of two upright stones supporting a capstone. Its particular interest is that it is alien to the surviving Great Stone architecture of the Ridgeway, but strikingly similar to many of the dolmens in Cornwall, indicating the immense spread of Great Stone culture at its height. Did some notable man from Cornwall die on a pilgrimage to Avebury, to be commemora-

ted by his family with a dolmen in their own tradition? Were there once many such dolmens round the Ridgeway, the rest broken by millennia of weathering and the plough? One cannot know. This lonely monument is strangely moving. One returns to the surging traffic of the A4 knowing that every one of its cars and lorries will be obsolete in ten years, but here on the hillside is a piece of man's handiwork that has endured for forty centuries.

Avebury

Distances from Avebury	
Perambulation of the Avebury Great Circle	¾ mile
Avebury to Overton Hill	1¼ miles
Overton Hill to Wansdyke	2 miles
Along Wansdyke to Allington Down	2½ miles
Allington Down to Overton Hill	3 miles
Overton Hill to Avebury	1¼ miles
From A4 to West Kennett Long Barrow (on foot)	½ mile
Return to A4	½ mile
Main road to Devil's Den and back	1¼ miles
Total	13 miles

The walking distance can be reduced by 2½ miles by driving from Avebury to Overton Hill (where there is a lay-by).

Avebury to Silbury Hill	on foot	approx. 1 mile
	by car	2½ miles

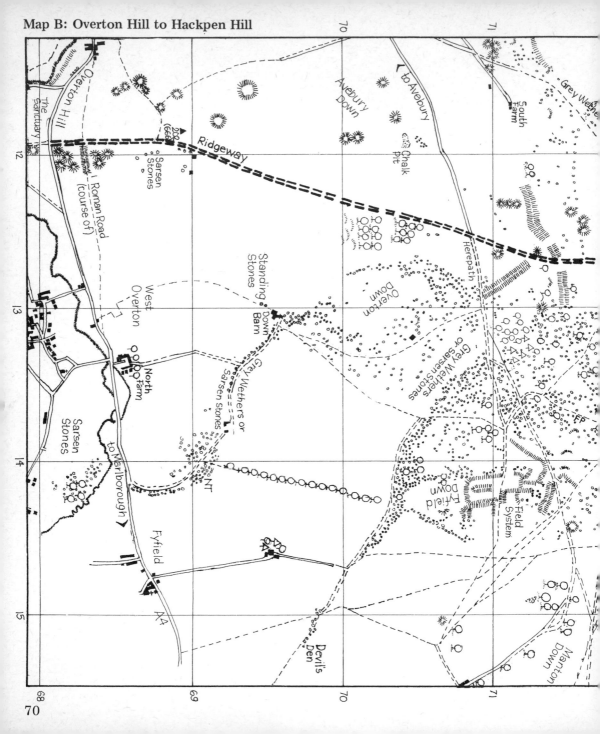

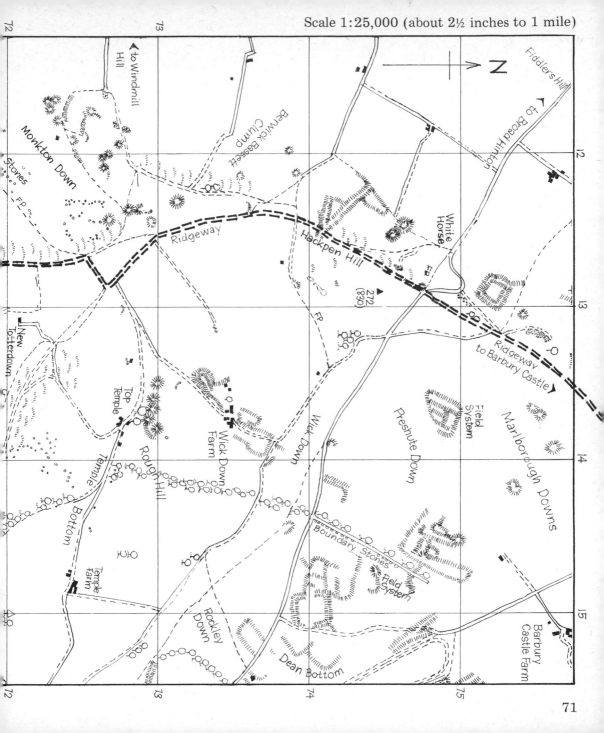

Scale 1:25,000 (about 2½ inches to 1 mile)

N

to Windmill Hill

Monkton Down

Stones

FP

Berwick Bassett Clump

Fiddlers Hill

to Broad Hinton

White Horse

12

Ridgeway

Hackpen Hill

FP

13

272 (830)

FP

New Totterdown

Ridgeway to Barbury Castle

Top Temple

Wick Down Farm

Wick Down

Preshute Down

Field System

Marlborough Downs

14

Rough Hill

Temple Bottom

Boundary Stones

Field System

Temple Farm

Rockley Down

Barbury Castle Farm

15

Dean Bottom

72   73   74   75

71

3 The Climb from the Sanctuary

Dewpond on Fyfield Down

118681

The Ridgeway Path of the Countryside Commission's continuous walk to Streatley starts across the road from The Sanctuary on Overton Hill. It begins to climb Avebury Down appropriately enough between two groups of barrows, and as you climb you can see numerous examples of these strange inverted-bowl-like tombs (the Ordnance Survey's 'tumuli') to both sides of the path.

Writing about a hundred years ago, Richard Jefferies (1848-1887) described the Ridgeway thus:

A broad green track runs for many a long, long mile across the Downs, now following the ridges, now winding past at the foot of a grassy slope, then stretching away through cornfield and fallow. It is distinct from the wagon-tracks which cross it here and there, for these are local only, and if traced up land the wayfarer presently in a maze of fields, or end abruptly in the rickyard of a lone farmhouse. It is distinct from the hard roads of modern construction which also at wide intervals cross its course, dusty and glaringly white in the sunshine. It is not a farm track: you may walk for twenty miles along it over the hills; neither is it the King's highway . . . Plough and harrow press hard on the ancient track, and yet dare not encroach upon it. With varying width, from twenty to fifty yards, it runs like a green ribbon . . . a width that allows a flock of sheep to travel easily side by side.*

Neither farm track nor King's highway . . . Jefferies's descrip-

*Richard Jefferies, *Wild Life in a Southern County* (Smith, Elder, London, 1879).

tion is exactly right. The Ridgeway is far older than either, and belongs not so much to people as to the whole human race

> For war, for water, or for better grain
> A thousand generations trod this way.
> Warmed by the sun, shivering in the rain —
> But progress for mankind, or so they say.*

To me, the main puzzle of the Ridgeway is that it has survived. How has it escaped the plough over thousands of years of close-fisted land-owning and jealous property rights? It has not, everywhere; away from these high Downs it can now be found in stretches only, the rest having vanished into farms and fields. But here, where the ancient road served the heart of the lost civilization that produced the Great Stone Culture, something has protected it, something more powerful than laws or charters, an atavistic fear perhaps. Jefferies, again, is right — 'Plough and harrow press hard . . . yet dare not encroach.' It is as if over thousands and thousands of years ordinary greedy men were brought up short by — what? A line of footsteps in the chalky mud? A feeling that a road trodden by countless generations has established property rights of its own? A simpler sense, felt in the bowels rather

Barrow on the Ridgeway above Avebury

than the mind, that to plough the Ridgeway would exact retribution from the ghosts of all those years? I do not know. The fact is that the Ridgeway on these Downs *has* remained unploughed, a right of way established for the human race by laws older than any writ of man. It is curiously comforting that a basic need of man — the right to walk over the hills — should be so respected just because it *is* a basic need.

The Ridgeway became a road because it is a route over high chalk uplands where men can see where they are going. The Downs now are bare, and have been for three thousand years at least. Were they always so? Trees will grow on these uplands — thorn, ash, and the pines that look alien now but may not always have been so. It is certain, I think, that the high

*J.R.L. Anderson, *The Upper Thames* (Eyre & Spottiswoode, London 1970, revised edition Eyre Methuen, London, 1974).

Downs can never have been so densely wooded as the coombes and river valleys. Man must have been led to walk upon them because the going was easier than below the spring line. But ease of travel is relative; because prehistoric man found it easier to walk the Ridgeway than the lower routes does not mean that the Ridgeway was as clear of obstructions as it is now. Man has been changing the landscape for ten thousand years at least. It may have needed centuries of flint axe work and laboriously kindled fire to make much impression on the woodland of the high Downs, but the centuries passed. Later, when the Neolithic farmers brought pigs to these Downs, the rooting habits of the pig achieved probably more clearance in decades than man alone could accomplish in centuries. Man and the pig between them cleared the Downs, and the sheep carried on the process.

The width of the Ridgeway is another puzzle: it is not a footpath but a road, as wide as, in places wider than, many modern roads. I put this down to the probability that throughout its history it was a path not merely for man, but for his animals too: the long-horned ox *(bos primigenius)* brought by the first farmers in their hazardous small-boat voyages to establish the first herds of cattle in England; the later (much more useful) *bos longifrons*; the pigs, the sheep, the horses bred from small wild ponies. The Ridgeway was a highway for all of them and their owners, whether they were fleeing from raiders, or themselves on raiding expeditions to find new land to colonize. Refugees, colonists and landowners of later generations have respected the Ridgeway as a highway of their own past.

The survival of the Ridgeway is all the more remarkable in that for the past thousand years or so it has not led anywhere in particular except to the high Downs. With the exception of East Kennett, and possibly Chiseldon, near Swindon, where for a short stretch the Ridgeway has been incorporated in a modern road, there are no villages directly on it; villages grew in the valleys, and the roads serving them followed lower contours than the austere route of the Ridgeway. Roads normally survive because they are useful, as many Roman

Looking back towards
Avebury from the Ridgeway

roads remain to carry motor traffic today. The Ridgeway's general usefulness as a highway belonged to an era before the villages, and ended with it. It is still useful to farmers for their tractors, but there are local farm tracks as-well, and there is now no particular need of the Ridgeway as a continuous route. Yet it has survived: one can but accept the fact, and be thankful for it.

Richard Jefferies's century-old description of the Ridgeway is still good, though tractors have made the path less green than it was for him. There are still stretches of green turf sward, but more on the White Horse Downs than on the Marlborough Downs. At the Avebury end it is distinctly rutted and rough, and in anything but the driest of weather you may have to pick your way. This is not necessarily a disadvantage: you will see more little things — the ants that so delighted Jefferies, nodules of flint that would have been worth picking up five thousand years ago. There have been two major chromatic changes since he wrote, one sharp, one less so. The sharp change is in the colour of the Ridgeway's rare junctions with his 'modern' roads, 'glaringly white in the sunshine'. The same country roads are now black or grey, surfaced with bitumen and less dusty than they were when he knew them. The other colour change is more pervasive, deriving from the far greater acreage of Downland that it has become profitable to plough. There was some ploughland in Jefferies's day, so the change here is of degree rather than kind; nevertheless, it is a major change, adding many more squares of patchwork-quilt to the landscape. It can be breathtakingly beautiful — an immense sweep of chequered landscape, the green of the turf spreading like inlets of a green sea between the capes and bays of the ploughed land, in every shade of beige and brown, from the near-white of chalk topsoil to the darker browns where there is more clay. I like this landscape best when it is newly ploughed, with the bones of the land still hard and bare. In summer, when sown fields are ripening you get a richer, but to me less satisfying, effect. But some think the ripple of growing corn or freshly sown grass the lovelier picture. It is of no matter; the beauty is in the land, whatever its dress.

118681   From the start at Overton Hill (170 metres or nearly 560 feet) you climb fairly steeply to 202 metres (663 feet) in the first half mile. The next mile is more undulating, but still a climb, taking you to about 229 metres (741 feet), where you meet the track, marked on the old one-inch map as the

125708   *herepath*, coming up from Avebury. An east-going track also joins the Ridgeway here, and if you have time it is worth digressing for a mile or so, for this track takes you into the

Sarsen on Fyfield Down

80

Nature Reserve of Fyfield Down, described by Peter Fowler, one of the leading archaeologists of Wessex, as the 'best preserved accessible large tract of ancient landscape in Wessex'.* Fyfield Down is also believed to be the source of the sarsen stones used in the construction of Stonehenge, to which they had to be dragged on tree-trunk rollers over twenty miles.

Within an area of some four square miles of Overton Down and Fyfield Down there is visible evidence of man's efforts to earn a living over five thousand years, of how he lived, and of how he buried his dead. For ten years (1959-68) Peter Fowler conducted systematic excavation of a number of selected sites in the locality, adding substantially to our knowledge of prehistory, and of the often almost equally shadowy centuries of the Dark and Middle Ages. Among his more important discoveries were three small *flat* cemeteries of the Beaker period, particularly interesting in an area so rich in elaborate barrow-tombs. The barrows themselves and the vast works at Avebury and Silbury Hill imply a population of considerable size. Demographic studies of prehistoric peoples must necessarily be guesswork — we have no means of knowing the composition in terms of age groups, except that it seems safe to assume that infant mortality was high, and that relatively few people lived into their sixties. Given that rather more than half the population were women, and assuming that perhaps one quarter of the male population were too young or too old (or unfit) for heavy work, the five hundred people needed to work on Silbury Hill represent a population of around fourteen hundred at least — larger still if the higher estimates of the Silbury workforce are used. And that assumes that every able-bodied man could be available for Silbury, which is, of course, absurd. In addition to the work force for Silbury there must have been a labour force several times as large to provide food for the construction workers on the earthwork. We cannot estimate how many men and women were required to feed five hundred construction workers, for we have no means of assessing the productivity of Neolithic agriculture four thousand years ago. It could

*P.J. Fowler, *Wessex* (Regional Archaeologies, Heinemann Educational Books, London, 1967).

scarcely have been high: moreover, manpower would also be required for defence, and there would be a number of specialists — men skilled in the making of stone tools and bone shovels, overseers, priests and their attendants. It is hard to see how works on the scale of Silbury Hill and the Great Circle at Avebury could have been accomplished without a local population of fifteen to twenty thousand, possibly considerably more. Where did they live? Where are their remains?

The barrows, numerous as they are, house but a tiny fraction of the (presumably) more eminent dead; even assuming that many more barrows have disappeared, the barrow-graves cannot possibly account for a human population on the scale that must have existed in this part of the Ridgeway country-side when it was the metropolitan area of a major civilization. Peter Fowler's discovery of non-barrow cemeteries from the period of barrow-burial is an important indication of a work-ing population which could neither afford (nor, perhaps, be considered eligible for) barrow-graves.

But where did they live? Fyfield Down, with its little fields scratched out of the hillside with wooden digging-sticks undoubtedly supported some Neolithic and Beaker families, but it could not have supported many. It is hard to reconcile the high degree of organization required for works on the scale of Avebury and Silbury with a scattered population of peasant pastoralists and farmers; but nothing has ever come to light to indicate towns even remotely comparable with the cities of other ancient civilizations. Some would hold that I am wrong to call the Great Stone Culture a civilization — it had no writing, and has left nothing like the legacies of Mesopotamia and Egypt. All this is true, but what is civiliza-tion? It is impossible to contemplate the monuments of the Great Stone Culture without feeling that these were the work of men with imagination and skills that raised them far above the animal level of human existence. They could not, or did not, build in masonry, but some believe that the design of Stonehenge, and perhaps of other Great Stone monuments, embodies mathematical knowledge of a high order. Certainly the axis of Stonehenge seems to be aligned on fairly exact astronomical observation, to compute the points of sunrise and sunset on the longest and shortest days of the year. Whether the stones are so positioned as to form a kind of Megalithic computer which could be used to predict eclipses must remain speculation, if only because Stonehenge as it now stands is lacking many of its original stones. Enough remain, however, to testify — as Avebury and Silbury Hill

testify — to the engineering skill of the vanished people who could design and build such monuments. The transport alone of the Great Stones would tax the skill of modern civil engineers, with all their resources of cranes, low-loaders, powerful machinery and metalled roads.

Professor Atkinson's guide to Stonehenge and Avebury has an admirable section, with clear drawings, reconstructing the methods by which a primitive people with no resources other than manpower, rawhide and wood might have been able to move stones weighing many tons across the rough country of the Marlborough Downs, or in the case of the 'Blue Stones' of Stonehenge, from the Prescelly Mountains north-east of Milford Haven, over a land and sea route not far short of two hundred and fifty miles (about four hundred kilometres). However you reconstruct this route it must involve a sea-crossing (presumably by raft, for one cannot envisage any other vessel of the period capable of carrying such weight) across the Bristol Channel, and then either a long stretch of land-haulage, or a complex mixture of land-haulage and rafting up rivers. In reading accounts of such performances in anti-quity, it is all too easy to dissolve the mystery and to say, 'Oh yes, of course — that must be how they did it!' If you consider the undertaking a little longer, the awe returns. The Bristol Channel is a formidable seaway, and to navigate an unhandy raft, liable to be half-waterlogged with a heavy cargo, from Milford Haven to the Bristol shore, calls for skill and determination that seem almost superhuman. So with shifting massive blocks of stone on unturned rollers: tree trunks will roll, and no doubt it can be done, but the order of foreman-ship over, and obedience in, the hauling-crew strains belief. The skills, determination and obedience must have been there — but they could not be found in a community of scattered peasants. I think the Great Stone Culture of the Ridgeway countryside *must* be called a civilization, with priests, kings and dynasties, traditions, laws and learned men that remain real however impenetrable the oblivion that covers them.

But why did these people who could do such marvellous things with Great Stones not *build* in stone? Some of the things they did not do are as mystifying as those they did. They could, and did, build drystone walling for their tombs; why did not their great men, who could command so many other skills, use blocks of stone for palaces? Timber was plentiful in the valleys and at least on the lower slopes of the Downs, and felling trees for timber would serve the double purpose of clearing land for sowing. We know that there were wooden houses, because a few sites with post-holes for apparently circular wooden dwellings have been found. Perhaps there was a tradition — or an edict — that stone was for the gods and for great men who might become gods on death, but that the living must make do with wood.

But the slight evidence of wooden round houses that has come to light gives no indication of towns. Were there ever any more or less urban settlements, and if so, where? No one yet knows — I write 'yet' because no one can say what future archaeology may reveal. The degree of social organization required for the communal engineering of the Great Stone Culture would seem to call for town centres of some sort, but none has yet been found. This is but one of the mysteries of these mysterious people.

Fyfield Down is dotted with sarsens, groups of which are marked on the map with their old name 'Grey Wethers'. At a little distance they do indeed resemble flocks of sheep — many times I have needed field glasses to determine whether a hillside is covered by sheep or stones.

The field system around map reference 142708 is an interesting study. These 'field systems' marked as antiquities on the map are often called 'Celtic fields', but the name is misleading. It derives from a simplistic theory that because there are Celtic peoples in Cornwall, Wales and Scotland, and because groups of Ancient Britons pushed out by invading Romans and Saxons took refuge in those (then) wild places, all Ancient Britons must have been Celts. Precisely who the Celts were, and where they came from, are still matters of conjecture and dispute. What might be called the historical Celts appear to have derived from a people living around

Hallstatt in Austria in the first millennium B.C., who developed a remarkable skill with metals (the Hallstatt culture) and became the finest iron-workers in Europe. Around the sixth century B.C., they broke out of their homeland, and by reason of their tough fighting qualities and superior iron swords they managed to subjugate large tracts of France, Western Germany and the Low Countries. They do not seem to have invaded England in any numbers then, but some apparently came to try their luck as settlers, for from about the fifth century B.C. there is evidence of Celtic influence here. The Belgic tribes that invaded Southern England in the century or so before the Roman occupation were a mixture of Celtic and Teutonic stock, and most of the Celtic strain in the pre-Roman population of the Ridgeway countryside appears to have come with them, and is thus relatively recent.

The Belgic invaders are thought to have brought iron ploughs superior to anything the earlier inhabitants possessed, and the little, squarish fields cut on the Downs were once supposed to have been the work of these (Celtic) ploughmen. But it is now known that some of these fields date back to a period long before the Belgic invasions, and that others are post-Roman. Neolithic farmers with digging-sticks won fields for themselves, and later conquerors simply carried on with the work. The excavations at Fyfield have revealed successive layers of field systems more or less superimposed on one another over a span of about a thousand years from the early Iron Age to late Roman-British times; and a medieval English farm was found nearby! For all the expertise of modern archaeology in devising ways to date even marks on the earth, my own feeling here is of simple wonder at the continuity of human existence in one place. And thanks to the Nature Conservancy Council and the landowners who have entered into agreements with it to establish Nature Reserves, one can see Fyfield Down much as it was four thousand years ago. Not quite as it was, for man has been at work here all the time, but you can see what he had to work with. There were no barrow-graves before men made them, and there was more woodland at the time the graves began to appear. Piety raised the barrows over the community's distinguished dead, and hard work slowly thinned the woodland — you can see one of the 'sharpening stones' where the cutting edges of stone axes were renewed. But the man or woman going to work in the little fields at daybreak thousands of years ago saw the same general picture of the Downs that one can see here now: the peppering of sarsen stones, the rough grass of the steeper hill-side, the same arching sky.

From the crossing of the Avebury-Fyfield tracks, the Ridge-way again climbs steeply, and in the next half-mile reaches 254 metres (832 feet). Due west of the Ridgeway at this spot, just over two miles away across the steep coombe of the headwaters of the Kennet, is Windmill Hill. On the top of this hill (187 metres, 613 feet) are three concentric rings of banked earth raised at some time during the centuries between about 3000-2500 B.C. to form one of the earliest tribal or religious meeting places of the Neolithic settlers in the Ridgeway countryside. It is about a mile and a half north-west of Avebury and in the same metropolitan complex, but it is older than the Great Stone meeting place or temple there.

087714

The Windmill Hill site was carefully excavated about fifty years ago, and provided important evidence of the degree of culture reached by the forerunners of the builders of Avebury and Stonehenge — so important that they are now known as the people of the 'Windmill Hill Culture'. They do not appear to have made their homes on Windmill Hill, for no trace of buildings that might have been houses has been found there. But much archaeological evidence came to light of pilgrims or visitors to the place: they seem to have camped and cooked in the ditches, leaving behind them bits of broken pottery and the bones of animals from their meals — not untidily as scattered litter but, it would seem, deliberately buried and put out of sight. (A Stone Age lesson in good manners!) Professor Atkinson suggests that these relics may have been the remains of ceremonial feasts — a reasonable interpreta-tion, for remnants of food perhaps blessed and considered sacred might well be formally buried, and the pottery may have contained offerings of some sort. Finds from the Wind-mill Hill excavations are in the Avebury Museum.

Again we have evidence of communal life and social organization going back far into prehistory. It shows that the flowering of the Great Stone civilization perhaps a thousand years later (2000-1600 B.C.) had deep roots, and that the Beaker people who brought the culture to its peak of refinement did not start from nothing, but found much in the way of ordered society here when they came.

There is one important qualification, though, to be made of all interpretations of early life on the Downs — in the millennia that have gone by since Neolithic times it is estimated that something like two feet of the chalk surface of the Downs has been weathered away. This does not belittle the evidence that remains — rather, it enhances it, for if so much remains, how much more may have been lost? The remains of wooden buildings, requiring nothing much in the way of foundations may have disappeared literally into thin air, but this is not quite enough to resolve the perplexity that most of the people who created the Great Stone Culture apparently lived nowhere: man is known by his rubbish, and many of the archaeological treasures in museums now come from the rubbish dumps of earlier centuries. Much human rubbish (alas for the twentieth century, but happily for the archaeologist) is almost indestructible: bits of potsherd, bones, worn out stone tools outlast millennia. Therefore, although traces of wooden huts or houses may have vanished into thin air, the human refuse from such settlements would not necessarily vanish with them. Much may have been lost under the plough before anyone thought of protecting sites of archaeological interest; the ploughshares of centuries will grind most things into fragments.

Richard Jefferies — it must be remembered that he was writing a hundred years ago — describes the attitude of a ploughman near the Ridgeway on turning up a pottery 'jar', perhaps three thousand years old. He writes without condemnation, recording an incident with gently nostalgic interest:

Prehistoric sharpening stone on Fyfield Down

Above, on the summit, is another ancient camp, and below two more turf-grown tumuli, low, and shaped like an inverted bowl. Many more have been ploughed down, doubtless, in the course of the years: sometimes still as the share travels through the soil there is a sudden jerk, and a scraping sound of iron against stone. The ploughman eagerly tears away the earth and moves the stone, to find a jar, as he thinks — in fact a funeral urn. Like all uneducated people, in the Far East as well as in the West, he is imbued with the idea of finding hidden treasure, and breaks the urn in pieces to discover —

nothing; it is empty. He will carry the fragments home to the farm, where, after a moment's curiosity, they will be thrown away with potsherds and finally used to mend the floor of the cowpen. *

As late as 1880 people at Avebury digging a hole to put up a flagstaff for a village fete dug up a pottery jar or beaker. They put it on a wall and invited children to throw stones at it: 'Not one sherd survived.'†

So much has gone. But as much more, perhaps, remains to be found. In all attempts to understand the past we must qualify our questions by trying to understand the realities of the present. This does not lessen the awe and mysteries of the past, but helps, perhaps, to keep our questioning on the right side of humility.

NOTE: the approach to Windmill Hill is not from this part of the Ridgeway, though it is possible to descend the chine to the valley, cross the Avebury-Swindon road about half a mile south of Winterbourne Monkton, and follow a track to the hill from the west side of the main road. An easier approach is by road via Avebury Trusloe, about half a mile west of Avebury itself.

As it nears the top of Monkton Down, overlooking Winterbourne Monkton and Windmill Hill, the Ridgeway Path makes a dog-leg turn to the east, and two hundred yards further on a sharp turn back to the north. A number of other tracks meet it here, but the Ridgeway is signposted, and you can avoid the trouble that Richard Jefferies warns against, of wandering off along false trails that lead nowhere. (Though one of the footpaths here offers a pleasant walk of between four and five miles to Marlborough.)

128727

The Ridgeway proper climbs on towards Hackpen Hill, running near the crest of a steep scarp falling sharply to the west

*Richard Jefferies, *Wild Life in a Southern County*.

†D. Emerson Chapman, *Is This Your First Visit to Avebury?* (H.M. Stationery Office, London, 1947).

Hackpen Horse

— a hillside that brings to mind C.E. Montague's vivid phrase about contours being so close that they seem to sing together. On the side of Hackpen Hill (though you can't see it from the Ridgeway, because you are above it) is the Hackpen White Horse, cut in the chalk after the style of (but much more recent than) the famous White Horse at Uffington, which we shall meet later. The Hackpen White Horse is of no great antiquity, having been cut to please an antiquarian fancy in the nineteenth century. There are, or were (for the grass grows quickly over hill figures unless they are regularly scoured) nine or ten of these eighteenth- and early nineteenth-century White Horses on the Downs. Though relatively modern, they have, as Jacquetta Hawkes puts it, 'a link with antiquity because they were sired by the White Horse of Uffington'. They were harmless enough follies of a period when labour was cheap, and they were not necessarily wholly selfish expressions of some landowner's whim, for such ideas were sometimes kindly ways of finding work for farmhands who would otherwise have been out of a job, and (before the Welfare State) on parish relief or tramping from workhouse to workhouse. The days of private follies — like the splendid folly at Abingdon of a ruined church *built as ruins* to give a romantic touch to a garden near the site of a vanished Benedictine Abbey — are over. We have replaced them with communal follies like blocks of tower flats and unnecessary airports. Progress, no doubt, though the gain is not immediately obvious.

A mile or so beyond the dog-leg turn you are more or less on the summit ridge of Hackpen, at about 270 metres (886 feet) For the next two miles on to Barbury Castle the path keeps to the ridge, rising and falling with the run of the land, but staying near the 259-metre (850-foot) contour. The sky is part of the landscape, seeming to touch it, and every foot-step opens up a slightly different view of the never-changing, always subtly changing, countryside of the high Downs. For all its antiquity, much of it — and here for the better — is man-made. Long, sweeping hillsides which might otherwise seem sometimes rather bleak are given focus and humanity by clumps of trees, usually beech, planted here and there as windbreaks. The thorn, generally wizened and alone, is the natural tree of this high country, fairy-like when in blossom, but for most of the year looking a little forlorn. Man, for the most part eighteenth-century man, brought the beech trees, and they have taken to the countryside as if they were living sarsens. These beech coppices are a glory of the landscape now, and they are worth a closer look. They are not the cathedral-like beechwoods of Savernake or Burnham, rather they are cottage-style beeches. They have had to struggle to survive, but just as the finest wines come from vines that have fought for survival on thin soils, so these beech coppices on the high Downs have a distinction of their own, humbler than the majesty of beech trees in grand avenues, but more individual and somehow kindlier. They are usually marked on the map, and are helpful signposts for orienting oneself, as well as a delight to look at.

This is glorious walking country, even in rain, which (unless you are unlucky enough to choose a really vile day) is soft and refreshing, as rain in town streets never seems to be. On a fine day the air is magical, tingling in nostrils and lungs and giving a lift like a lark's wing. You walk free, revelling in the stride that has kept man going through the centuries, feeling with John Davidson the sheer intoxication of going on:

> *O long before the bere was steeped for malt*
> *And long before the grape was crushed for wine*
> *The glory of a march without a halt*
> *The triumph of a stride like yours and mine*
> *Was known to folk like us who walked about*
> *To be the sprightliest cordial out and out!*
> *Folk like us with hearts that beat,*
> *Sang it too, in sun and rain —*
> *'Heel and toe from dawn to dusk,*
> *Round the world and home again.'**

On the way to Barbury, about a mile and a half before you reach the great hill-fort called Barbury Castle, the Ridgeway is crossed by a metalled road, a minor road from Marlborough

129747

*John Davidson,'The Last Journey'.

92

to Broad Hinton, where it becomes B4041 to Wootton Bassett. You don't take this road, but it is useful to remember as an access route to a village (Broad Hinton is just under two miles away). I am writing of the Ridgeway as a continuous walk, but have not forgotten the logistics of modern living: I shall discuss meeting places, transport and car-ferrying in a later chapter.

Fyfield Down

Distances from Overton to Barbury Castle	
Overton to Avebury-Fyfield crossways	1¾ miles
Fyfield Down diversion and return to the Ridgeway	3 miles
Avebury crossways to Barbury Castle	4 miles
Total	8¾ miles

Map C1: Barbury Castle to Whitefield Hill

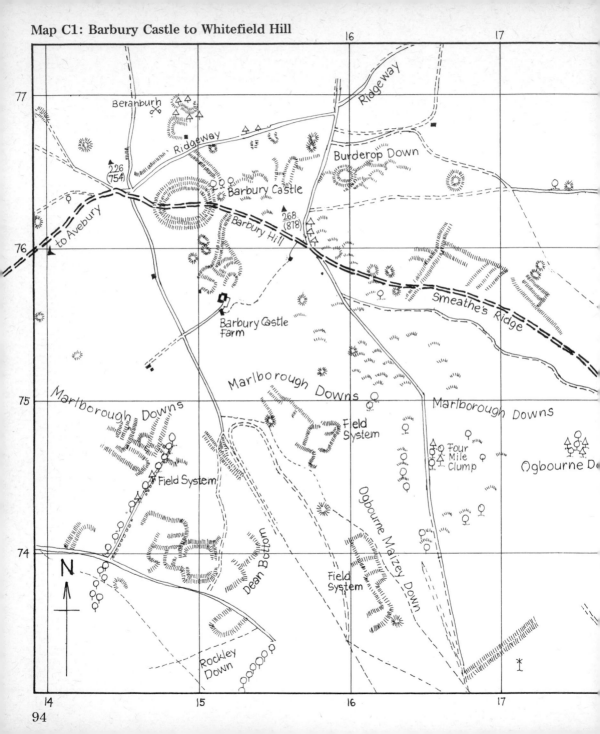

Beranburh

Ridgeway

Ridgeway

Burderop Down

226
(754)

to Avebury

Barbury Castle

Barbury Hill

268
(878)

Smeathe's Ridge

Barbury Castle
Farm

Marlborough Downs

Marlborough Downs

Marlborough Downs

Field
System

Four
Mile
Clump

Ogbourne D

Field System

Ogbourne Maizey Down

Dean Bottom

Field
System

N

Rockley
Down

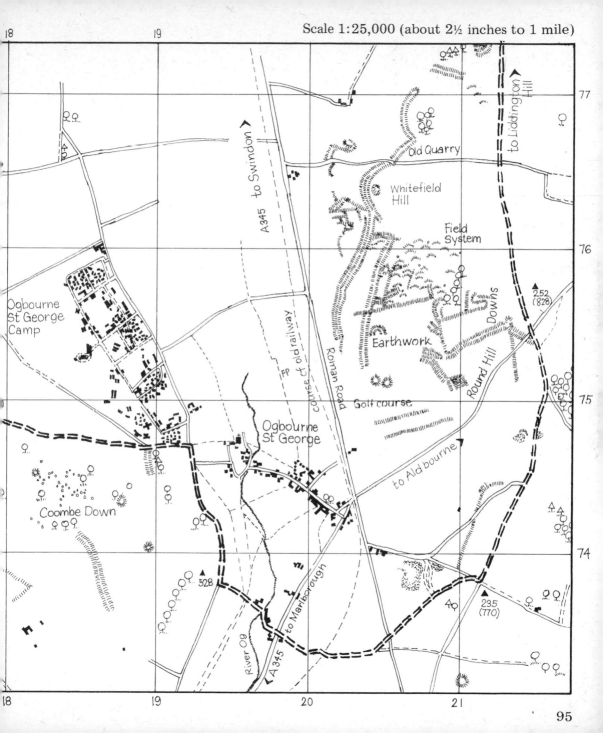

Scale 1:25,000 (about 2½ inches to 1 mile)

to Liddington Hill

Old Quarry

Whitefield Hill

Field System

A345 to Swindon

Round Hill Downs

252 (828)

Earthwork

Course of old railway

FP

Roman Road

Golf course

Ogbourne St George Camp

Ogbourne St George

to Aldbourne

Coombe Down

528

River Og

A345 to Marlborough

235 (770)

95

Map C2: Whitefield Hill to Foxhill

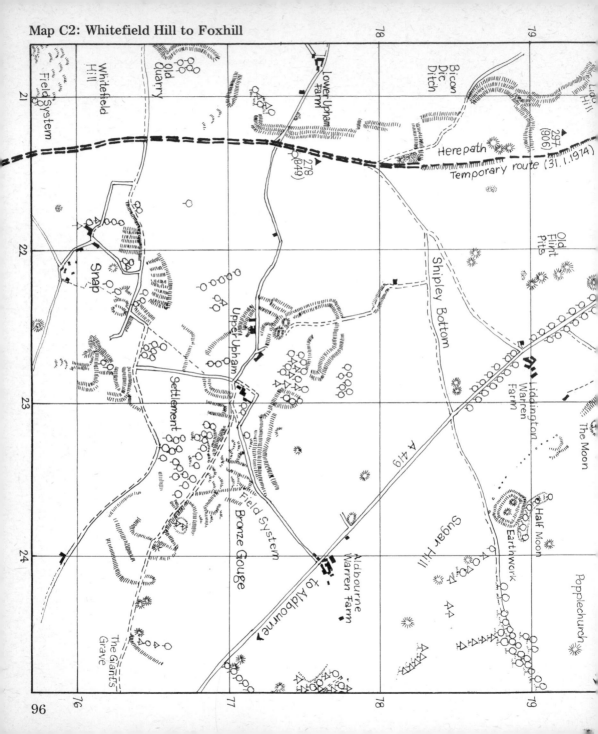

78

79

Bicon Dic Ditch

Lidar Hill

Lower Upham Farm

21

Field System

Whitefield Hill

Old Quarry

▲ 297 (906)

▲ 278 (849)

Herepath

Temporary route (31.1.1974)

Old Flint Pits

22

Snap

Shipley Bottom

Upper Upham

The Moon

23

Settlement

Field System

A 419

Liddington Warren Farm

Half Moon

Earthwork

Bronze Gouge

Sugar Hill

Popplechurch

24

The Giant's Grave

to Aldbourne

Aldbourne Warren Farm

76

77

78

79

96

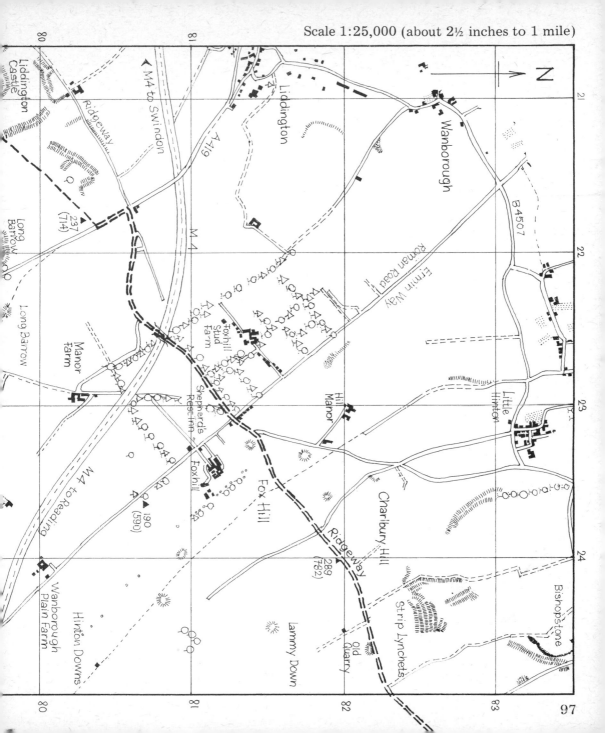

N

Liddington Castle

Ridgeway

M4 to Swindon

A419

Liddington

Wanborough

B 4507

Long Barrow

237 (714)

Long Barrow

M4

Ermin Way

Roman Road

22

Manor Farm

Foxhill Stud Farm

Shepherd's Rest Inn

Hill Manor

Little Hinton

23

Foxhill

190 (590)

Fox Hill

M4 to Reading

Charlbury Hill

Ridgeway

289 (782)

Strip Lynchets

Bishopstone

Wanborough Plain Farm

Hinton Downs

Lammy Down

Old Quarry

24

80

81

82

83

97

4 The First of the Forts

What happened to the Great Stone civilization no one knows. It seems to have reached its peak around 1600-1500 B.C., but must have continued to flourish for another 300-400 years, for the final reconstruction of Stonehenge is dated at around 1300 B.C. The remarkable discovery at Stonehenge as recently as 1953 of the carved outlines of what seems to be an early Bronze Age dagger and some bronze axe-heads suggests that the region remained a place of cultural pilgrimage until towards the end of the second millennium B.C. The dagger resembles the workmanship of Minoan Crete or Mycenean Greece, and the axe-heads seem similar to those made by the early bronze smiths in Ireland (before the Celts, perhaps the finest metal workers in Western Europe) from about the middle of the second millennium. Those Irish axes were much valued, and archaeologists have found evidence of an export trade in them to various parts of Britain and continental Europe. To retain links with the Mediterranean world and Ireland implies a continuing importance for the Great Stone region — religious probably, but no doubt economic as well, for pilgrims were great spreaders of trade.

But the importance of the region dwindled. There is no evidence that the Great Stone civilization met its end in any catastrophic war. Stonehenge, Avebury, the great barrows and hosts of monuments in the region were not thrown down by conquerors; rather, they were left alone to weather and decay. The Beaker people, imaginative, enterprising and ingenious, slipped out of history as mysteriously as they entered it — save that their blood must continue to pulse in many of us still: one can see, perhaps, Beaker characteristics in some of the enterprises that made Britain great in the Victorian era. Did their civilization simply exhaust itself, with a succession of sons and daughters who were made soft by having too many slaves, and who were not nearly so enterprising as their fathers and mothers — as other civilizations have exhausted themselves? Were they destroyed by slow economic erosion, as bronze, which they once controlled as a rarity, became the stuff of everyday life? Wessex — the Ridgeway countryside — is poor in metallic ores. Its resources are good farmland, flint and stone. In their heyday, the Beaker aristocracy possessed a knowledge of bronze-working which set them apart from the rest of their community, a priestly knowledge, perhaps, which the gods shared only with a chosen few. When bronze swords, bronze kettles, bronze hairpins became available to anybody who could pay a few baskets of grain, did this priestly ascendancy evaporate? It may be so. Certainly for this, or for some other unguessed reason, the Great Stone Culture that had been dominant in the region for well over a thousand years began to diminish in the last quarter of the second millennium B.C. By the end of the millennium the Great Stones and the earthworks that went with them were museum pieces, as remote from the population of the countryside as the Babylonian relics in the British Museum are to the lunch-time crowds in Tottenham Court Road and Oxford Street.

'The four hundred years after 1000 B.C. is a virtual blank in the archaeology of Wessex,' writes Peter Fowler in his archaeological study of the region. Immigrants with Celtic metal-working skills related to the Hallstatt culture of Central Europe began to appear, but not in such numbers as to indicate an invasion; they were more like the Huguenots who came to England after the religious wars in France, immigrants who brought silk-weaving and other useful skills to seventeenth-century England, but who kept to themselves and exercised no political power in their new homeland. Gradually the influence and magnetic attraction of the once-metropolitan centre of the Great Stone Culture fell away, and there came generations who knew nothing of what the Great Stones meant. Since we do not know what gods were worshipped in the Great Stone temples, we know nothing of what deities replaced them — maybe the inhabitants of the Kennett Valley, the Vale of Pewsey and Salisbury Plain went through an age of scepticism and irreligion not dissimilar to that of our own era.

Some people must still have used the Ridgeway for had it remained untrodden for a thousand years it would scarcely exist as a road today. Later road-builders made roads on the lower contours, and did not follow the Ridgeway's austere and often inconvenient track, but somebody went on using the Ridgeway through those centuries: shepherds driving flocks, no doubt, who thus maintained the width of the Ridgeway as a drove road, and long-distance travellers from the south-west making for East Anglia, of whom there must always have been some, probably still found the old route a good one for bringing them to a convenient crossing of the Thames. But so little is known of this part of England in the early half of the first millennium B.C. that there is not much to speculate about. The next substantial milestones in time are the hill-forts.

They are uncertain milestones. They are called loosely 'Iron Age forts', but as the Iron Age in Wessex has no clear beginning, and the transition from bronze to iron — as from stone to bronze — certainly spread over centuries, the term is so nebulous as to be almost meaningless. Technically, hill-forts are divided into two main types: 'univallate', where an enclosure fortified by an earthen embankment is surrounded by a single ditch, and 'multivallate', where the enclosure has more than one surrounding ditch. It has been suggested that these two types represent forts built by different peoples, but I doubt if there is much in this. Where so little is known the desire to classify what can be seen is understandable, but whether a fort was embanked with one or more ditches may have been determined by the lie of the land and the labour immediately available. Moreover, it seems likely that some forts were extended over the years, as in later ages a castle might be extended by adding a tower or building a new wing.

It is very hard indeed to date a ditch. If you find weapons or bits of broken pottery thrown into it, it is reasonable to assume that the ditch was there for them to be thrown into; and if you can date the objects you can say that the ditch must have existed at that time. But you could not say how long the ditch had been dug before those particular objects were deposited in it. The hill-forts along the Ridgeway — in common with other hill-forts in Britain — are generally supposed to have been built from about 500 B.C. onwards, in the disturbed times that followed the waves of Celtic expansion in Western Europe. The Iron Age was brought to Britain, first with small groups of iron-working people who seem to have settled in Southern England more or less peacefully, then, in the last centuries before the Roman occupation, with powerful invasions by Belgic tribes from Caesar's Gaul. Caesar's expedition to Britain in 55 B.C. was really an extension of his campaigns in Gaul, and some of the Gallo-Celtic tribes which crossed to Britain just before him did so in an effort to escape the Roman legions.

Dating of the hill-forts generally to the Iron Age fits quite neatly into the framework of what is known of history, but it leaves much unexplained. The Beaker people and their Neolithic predecessors were adept at ditch-digging and earthmoving: why are they assumed to have built no fortifications? On Ram's Hill, which we shall pass, a hill-fort seems to have been built around an earlier enclosure constructed as early as 1500 B.C. The embanked ditches on Windmill Hill were earlier still — 3000 to 2500 B.C. These do not seem to have been fortifications, but the principle of fortifying a hill top by digging ditches round it is an obvious extension of such work.

I have never been happy about the attribution of the Ridgeway's forts to the confused late centuries of Gallo-Celtic invasion. Many of the smaller forts — there are about a hundred and fifty in Wessex alone — may indeed belong to this period; they are the equivalent of the moated farms of a later age when individuals had to protect themselves and their property as best they could. But the great forts along the Ridgeway — Barbury, Liddington, Uffington, Segsbury, and various supporting earthworks — are not like this; their siting suggests a coherent strategic purpose, requiring unified military command over a considerable area. The Beaker people in their heyday were clearly capable of a high degree of social organization, too. We know nothing of their wars, but it is unlikely that they never had to defend their civilization.

The Ridgeway forts are sited to command the Ridgeway itself, and to serve as defensive strong-points against attack from the north. The Ridgeway was an important trade route for the Beaker people and they needed to command it, not only to keep it open for themselves, but to deny its use to any hostile people seeking to approach their sanctuaries. Their cultural links with Brittany and the western seaboard of continental Europe may have enabled them to feel reasonably secure to the south: there may well have been more primitive peoples eager to try to raid them from the north. I do not think that archaeologists, rightly concerned with the physical relics of the past which they are trained to study, have paid enough attention to the political implications of the massive Ridgeway forts. Their siting, building and manning could not have been achieved without some centralized political power, and the Beaker period was the last in which there was anything approaching such power in England until the Roman occupation. The collapse of the Bronze Age civilization of the Great Stone Culture after about 1000 B.C. left no power capable of organized defence on the scale of the Ridgeway fortresses. And as defences against invasion from the Continent they point the wrong way — why construct fortifications facing north against an enemy coming up from the south?

No doubt the forts were used in various local wars during the centuries of the Iron Age, as they were certainly used nearly a thousand years later during the Saxon invasions. But I do not think they belong exclusively to the Iron Age. Excavation of some of the embankments has shown that in places at any rate they were revetted with sarsens — a Beaker touch, surely! The various Iron Age objects which have been found in the ditches may well have been brought by people taking refuge in the forts long after they were built.

148763   Barbury Castle, the first of the fortresses we meet on walking the Ridgeway from Overton, is a splendid specimen. It stands high, at some 268 metres (nearly 880 feet) on a great spur of the Downs overlooking the valley of the River Ray in which Swindon (five miles north of Barbury) has grown up. It is a magnificent position, protecting not only the routes from the

Barbury Castle

north to Avebury and Marlborough, but commanding the Ray valley. The Ray joins the Thames near Cricklade about eleven miles a little west of north of Barbury and any force attempting to advance southwards from the Thames here would have to reckon on outwitting or out-flanking the defenders of Barbury: reserves held at Barbury could be sent quickly into the valley to harry an enemy coming from the Thames. Just such a battle did take place in or about the year A.D. 556

when the remnants of the Romanized British were attempting
to repel the Saxons. It was fought on the slopes of Barbury
Hill about half a mile below the fortress. By this time,
however, the will to resist of the Roman-British inhabitants,
kindled to its last flame by Ambrosius and Arthur, had all
but flickered out, and whatever may have been the gallantry
of the last defenders of Barbury, the battle went against them.
It is recorded in the *Anglo-Saxon Chronicle* (compiled long
after the event) and the place is called *'Beran byrg'*,* from
which the name 'Barbury' derives. It means 'Bera's Hill', and
it may not be too fanciful to suppose that it commemorates
the name of the Saxon leader who won the battle. (The part

*Eilert Ekwall, *The Concise Oxford Dictionary of English Place Names*
(Oxford University Press, London, 1936, 4th edition 1960).

played by the hill-forts of the Ridgeway in the earlier, successful, campaign of Ambrosius against the Saxons is discussed in Chapter 5).

Barbury is peaceful now, an ideal place to sit and rest and think, or to eat a picnic lunch. The circular earth banks offer a sheltered lee from whatever wind may be blowing, and the grass is more comfortable than most cushions. The space within the fort is large, about eleven and a half acres, and it has traces of hut-circles, suggesting either that at some period it had a permanent garrison, or that there was once a village of some sort inside the fortifications. The main problem in considering the permanent garrisoning of these Ridgeway forts — a problem still more acute in contemplating them as fortified settlements — is the apparent lack of any water supply. They are high above the spring-line, and while there are springs here and there on the lower slopes, and rivulets in some of the chines, it would mean a climb of half a mile or so there and back to fetch water. To carry water in leather buckets over such a distance, enough for substantial numbers of people, would be an arduous job; furthermore, if there were enemies around, a water party would be exposed to attack. And an enemy in any numbers could quickly force a garrison to surrender by cutting off access to water, thus making the forts useless.

Barbury Castle ramparts

But such great fortifications would not have been built if they were useless. Therefore they must have had water, and a clue to the solution of the problem may be in the dew-ponds still to be found here and there on the high Downs. You pass one on the Ridgeway on the way up to Barbury. Some of these ponds may be quite modern. Richard Jefferies describes how they were made in his day to provide water for cattle: a shallow pit would be 'puddled' with a clay lining, and soot worked into the clay to discourage beetles and other boring insects which might otherwise make holes to let the water out. Once watertight, a dew-pond will gradually fill with water from the condensation of mist and low cloud, and, when filled, the water is slow to evaporate; it will, of course, be renewed whenever the right conditions for condensation

107

occur. Richard Jefferies thinks that the greater woodland cover of two, three, four thousand years ago would have aided precipitation from mist and cloud, and made dew-ponds more efficient in attracting and containing water. It is a sound scientific theory, even though Jefferies wrote without benefit of modern science. And since dew-ponds are shallow rather than deep — it is the *area* of condensation that matters — traces of them may be expected to have vanished with the weathering away of the chalk surface over the centuries. I am impressed by the folk-knowledge of the making of dew-ponds as recorded by Jefferies: the mixing of soot with clay to defeat boring insects seems to me to reflect the experience of antiquity. Given such ponds to supply water, the forts could have maintained themselves indefinitely, and I am sure that

All over the Ridgeway tree clumps dominate the skyline, visible for miles. As you draw near to one of them it is often concealed by the curve of a hill or the rampart of a fort. Then, as you round a corner it springs up at you with its leaves rattling in the wind . . .

that is how they managed. There is no need of such dew-ponds now; there are galvanized iron cattle-troughs on the Downs, supplied by pump. But given some catastrophe that denied petrol for the pumps, I daresay that the ancient technique for making dew-ponds would be remembered, and used.

The world of Richard Jefferies, for all that he was writing a mere century and not millennia ago, has gone. He writes of the Ridgeway:

Sometimes in the evening, when the wheat is nearly ripe, a shepherd lad will sit under the trees ... and as you pass along the track will come the mellow note of his wooden whistle,

from which poor instrument he draws a sweet sound. There is no tune — no recognizable melody: he plays from his heart, and for himself. In a room doubtless it would seem harsh and discordant; but there, the player unseen, his simple notes harmonize with the open plain, the looming hills, the ruddy sunset, as if striving to express the feelings these call forth.*

There are some sheep around the Ridgeway still, but not many, and few shepherds — one of the reasons for the disappearance of the sheep is the reluctance of twentieth-century wage-earners to accept the lonely life of a Downland shepherd. There is more money to be had in the motor factories of Oxford, Abingdon and Swindon. You will not now hear a

* *Wild Life in a Southern County.*

. . . from close up the individual trees separate from the mass . . .

shepherd playing a reed flute — a transistor radio is more
likely, though mercifully the Downs are big, and the
occurrence of people who want transistor radios as they walk
is fairly sparse. The weird economics of milk subsidies have
put cows on the Downs in place of sheep, a sight that seems
to me alien and sad in sheep country. But Neolithic and
Beaker farmers would have pastured cattle here if it had
profited them: one must beware of sentiment when meeting
the facts of life.

145764   A couple of hundred yards before reaching Barbury Castle,
the Countryside Commission decides to differ from prehistoric travellers about the precise route of the Ridgeway. The
ancient route — still marked on the modern Ordnance Survey

. . . and if you walk inside
the clump they close around
you

map — runs *north* of the fortress to make as directly as a
208796 Roman road for Liddington Hill, crowned with another fort,
some four and a half miles away. Because the Ridgeway
descends here, and is a direct route, some three or four miles
of it have been incorporated in a metalled road running past
193794 Chiseldon to cross first the Roman road from Swindon to
Marlborough (A345) and then the road from Swindon to
216806 Newbury (A419). The road system here is a palimpsest of

Original Ridgeway route
round Barbury Castle

civil engineering. The Romans mostly ignored the Ridgeway, because it ran too high and served none of their main centres of population, but here and there they used bits of it as feeder routes. The Swindon-Marlborough road is Roman, and three miles farther east the old Ridgeway crosses another major Roman road (Ermin Way) linking Cirencester with Newbury. A mile north-east of Liddington Hill the Ridgeway 226808 (which is metalled here) crosses the M4 motorway from London to Bristol by a bridge. Across the motorway the ancient route continues as a metalled road to Fox Hill, where 232813 it turns north-east for Bishopstone and Uffington, and becomes again an unmetalled drove road or walking track.

145764 The Countryside Commission's Ridgeway Path leaves the old Ridgeway just before Barbury Castle to run almost due east, by another ancient track, directly through the earthwork and on along a ridge known as Smeathe's Ridge to Ogbourne St 198734 George. Here it crosses the Swindon-Marlborough road, some four miles south of the ancient Ridgeway route, and then turns north to meet the old route again, via Round Hill Downs, a little to the east of Liddington Castle. It has to 217806 rejoin the metalled stretch of Ridgeway to Fox Hill in order to cross the motorway (M4).

Historically, this diversion has nothing to be said for it: the Ridgeway is making for the Thames, and the diversion, until it turns north again at Ogbourne St George, takes one back towards Marlborough. Practically, there is much in its favour: the descent by Smeathe's Ridge is one of the most beautiful stretches of the Marlborough Downs, and by following the Commission's route you avoid a rather dull stretch of nearly four miles of metalled road (adding, however, at least three miles to the walking distance from Barbury to Liddington). You also avoid having to overlook the rash of suburbs round Swindon. But the diversion, attractive as it is, distorts history by clouding the fact that the Ridgeway is older than the hillforts on it. The old road does not, indeed cannot, go through the fortress of Barbury Castle, because it follows the lip of the escarpment which the fort overlooks. At Liddington, too, the old road runs at the foot of the hill-fort and is overlooked by it, whereas the diversion approaches the fortress from the *south*. These forts were built to command the road, and to overawe the country to the *north* of it.

Half a mile east of Barbury Castle, following the Countryside Commission's route to Smeathe's Ridge and Ogbourne St George, the path meets a metalled minor road from Wroughton, three miles to the north. This road goes nowhere

157760

Elms at Ogbourne St George

Right On Round Hill Downs
Below Ruined railway bridge
across the Ridgeway at
Ogbourne St George

in particular, but simply runs up to the Downs, where it turns
into a track. Here there is a car park, where it may be useful
to know that there is a small building housing men's and
women's lavatories. Approaching Smeathe's Ridge the path
forks, the northerly branch leading on to the Ridge, the
southerly one going back to Marlborough.

Smeathe's Ridge descends in a rolling billow of Downland
from about 260 metres (853 feet) at the Barbury end to just
under 150 metres (592 feet) where it meets the Og valley.
The Og is a neat little river, giving its name to two villages,
Ogbourne St George and Ogbourne St Andrew, and joining
the Kennet at Marlborough. Smeathe's Ridge runs down to
the upper of the two villages, Ogbourne St George. The sign-

117

posted path skirts the village to the south, emerging on the
197734 Roman road to Marlborough. After crossing the road the
route winds round the village to the east to begin the climb
back towards Liddington by Round Hill Downs.

Ogbourne St George is a straggling village, and at the main
road end it is not particularly attractive. But it reaches nearly
a mile back into the Downs, and here there are some lovely
old houses among great trees, elms of the shape that really
does look immemorial and which, displayed on travel agents'
posters in New York, make the English countryside seem too
good to be true. One can be thankful that it still is real here
and there. If you feel like walking through a village after the
great open spaces of the Downs you can leave the path from
193747 Smeathe's Ridge on Coombe Down and take another path
leading directly to the village just south of a group of army
huts marked on the map as a camp. The camp is not beautiful,
but it is soon hidden by the hedges of a sunken lane and you
can enjoy the prettier bits of the village. On reaching the main
road turn right towards Marlborough, and you will pick up
the signposted Ridgeway route again about half a mile along
197734 the road.

The climb up Round Hill Downs runs roughly parallel with
the Roman road towards Swindon, about a mile to the east
of the road. After skirting a golf course you are back in the
familiar country of barrows and ancient field systems. The
path runs by the edge of the lovely woods of Aldbourne
Chase, and just north of the woods it crosses the metalled
215754 road from Ogbourne St George to Aldbourne, some three
miles along the road to the east. Aldbourne is a substantial
village or small country town, with banks and other such
amenities. There has been a good deal of new building round
it, but the heart of the place is old and beautiful, and
Aldbourne is a convenient resting place if you are spending
some days in the Ridgeway countryside.

Beyond the Aldbourne road you are soon on the 259-metre
(850-foot) contour again, on Whitefield Hill, and you meet a
213764 path running east towards a village still marked on the map as

Snap. But there is no village any longer, only the ghost of a place that was deliberately abandoned in the last century to make more room for sheep. The Highland Clearances in Scotland are described in all the history books: the dispossession of a few inarticulate peasants in Wiltshire was not on a sufficient scale to pull the national heartstrings. Yet it is sad that sheep should be deemed more profitable than men and women. Snap is an archaeological site now — the church, the

Not much remains of Snap

foundations of cottages, the alignment of the village street, nice subjects for a doctoral thesis. And perhaps a Victorian brooch or two will come to light to prove that women with lovers who gave them trinkets — out of a wage of seven shillings (35p) a week — once lived there.

Yet Snap had a long and interesting history. Its odd name does not figure in the *Oxford Dictionary of English Place-Names*, presumably because when the dictionary was first published in 1936 Snap had ceased to exist as a place. Yet the name deserves mention, for it seems to derive from a Viking word meaning a place of thin grazing for sheep (but the sheep won in the end) in an area where there was little Viking settlement. Did some eleventh-century Dane carve a holding for himself on these bare Downs? Well, he is one with the Romans and the Beaker folk now, awaiting the chance strike of an archaeologist's spade for anything ever to be known about him.

Ridgeway crossing the M4

208796

Two and a half miles on from the Snap crossways the path rejoins the metalled stretch of the old Ridgeway just to the east of Liddington Hill. The fort here is near the highest point of the Downs, standing at 277 metres (909 feet). It is a more formidable fortress than Barbury, partly because there is no easy footpath to it: you feel that invisible defenders still regard visitors as hostile. The Countryside Commission's path curls below it to the south, the old Ridgeway skirts it to the north, but no path invites you to the summit. You can get there by climbing the hillside, and once there you discover that the forbidding fortress has been loved, for a plate on the Ordnance Survey's concrete triangulation post records 'Liddington Hill, the hill beloved of Richard Jefferies and Alfred Williams.'

Richard Jefferies (1848-87), sometime reporter on the *North Wilts Herald* and author of some of the best pastoral writing in English, we have met before (see p.73). Alfred Williams (1877-1930) was a more local poet, his unpretentious verses about the Downs and the Wiltshire countryside giving immense pleasure to Wiltshire men and women. He was self-taught, having left school at eleven to work as odd-job boy on a farm. Later he got a job at the Great Western Railway Works in Swindon, which kept him going while he wrote his poetry. After a day's work as a hammer-man in the forge of the railway works he would go home to write verses, and with his wife, who must have been as remarkable as he was, to study Latin and Greek. Although by no means in good health, he volunteered for service in the First World War and was sent to India. There, as well as soldiering, he added Sanskrit to his study of languages. When he came home he acquired a tumble-down cottage at South Marston, on the outskirts of Swindon, which he and his wife restored and largely rebuilt themselves. They called it Ranikhet, after the depot where Alfred Williams had served in India: the name of the cottage in a Swindon suburb is an odd reminder of the British Raj, as vanished as the Roman Empire. In 1930, Alfred Williams was awarded a Civil List pension by Mr Ramsay MacDonald's Government, but he died before it could be paid to him. His widow died very soon after him. They are buried together in South Marston churchyard.

178829 Jefferies was born at Coate, also on the outskirts of Swindon, and three miles north-west of Liddington Hill. From the fort he could look down over the scene of his childhood, and the place inspired some of his finest writing. It occupies a superb position, scenically as well as strategically. Barbury commands the Ray valley; Liddington commands the Cole valley, east of Swindon, and the western end of the Vale of the White Horse. On a clear day you can see almost the whole valley of the Upper Thames from it.

From Liddington Hill you have no choice but to follow the metalled road that has here absorbed the Ridgeway to Foxhill

226808 — it is the only way to get across the motorway (M4) that now cuts through the Downs. The walk is no great hardship; it is a pleasant minor road, and it gives (to me, at any rate) a satisfying sense of detachment to stand on the bridge and watch the ceaseless traffic of the motorway scurrying under-

232813 neath. Moreover at the end of this stretch, at Foxhill, stands the only inn actually on the Ridgeway for the whole of its length, the Shepherd's Rest. It is a friendly place, and one feels that one has earned a drink there.

If you have arranged to meet a car at Foxhill, a diversion to Coate, the birthplace of Richard Jefferies, and Coate Water, which he made famous in *Bevis, the Story of a Boy*, is a pleasant bonus to this section of a Ridgeway walk. You can do it on foot from Liddington Hill, leaving the metalled stretch of the Ridgeway by a minor road to Badbury and going on through Badbury Wick, a walking distance of about three miles. But this is the outskirts of Swindon, now very much motorway and main-road country, and the trip is probably better made by car — from Foxhill the road journey is about five miles.

178829/176827

198796

At Coate the farmhouse where Richard Jefferies was born is preserved and it houses a museum containing a fascinating collection of manuscripts, first editions and letters relating both to Jefferies and to Alfred Williams. Across the main road into Swindon, a quarter of a mile or so south-west of Coate village, is Coate Water, a splendid lake nearly a mile long. This was originally a small natural lake, fed by a number of streamlets from the Downs. Early in the nineteenth century it was bought by the Wilts and Berks Canal Company and enlarged as a reservoir to provide water for the canal they had built to bring Somerset coal to Swindon, Wantage and other market towns in the two counties. The canal was never very prosperous, and with the coming of the Great Western Railway in the 1840s it fell on hard times. In Richard Jefferies's boyhood — wonderfully described in *Bevis* — Coate Water was a forgotten lake in a jungle of undergrowth, the haunt of wild birds and of adventurous small boys with home-made boats. In 1914 it was taken over by Swindon Corporation and has since been maintained as a beauty spot and inland water-resort. The corporation has done a good job. Coate Water is open all the year round for boating, fishing or just for the enjoyment of a placid sheet of water with beautiful walks all round it. The south-western end of the lake is a bird sanctuary, and the greater part of the lake is designated as a site of special scientific interest for observing the flocks of wild-fowl that congregate there, and the wild flowers, rarely to be found elsewhere in England, that survive in a lakeside habitat.

Distances from Barbury Castle to Foxhill	
Barbury to Liddington Hill, direct route along old Ridgeway	5 miles
Barbury to Ogbourne St George via Smeathe's Ridge	3 miles
Ogbourne St George to Liddington Hill via Round Hill Downs	5 miles
Diversion to Aldbourne and return	6 miles
Diversion to Snap	2 miles
Liddington Hill to Foxhill	2 miles
Diversion to Coate Water On foot from Liddington and return	6 miles
Perambulation of Coate village and lake	2 miles
By car from Foxhill and return	10 miles
Totals:	
Barbury to Foxhill direct route	7 miles
Barbury to Foxhill via Ogbourne St George	10 miles
With diversion to Snap	12 miles
With diversion to Aldbourne, omitting Snap	16 miles
Including Snap by shorter route from Aldbourne road	17 miles
Adding diversion to Coate (most conveniently by car)	27 miles

5   Diversion in Time –
Ambrosius and Arthur

I have described this book as a sort of four-dimensional guide
book, with signposts for travellers in time as well as in terres-
tial space. I have recommended various geographical diversions
from the Ridgeway and we might here, I think, make a
diversion in time, returning to the misty fifth century A.D.,
towards the end of which King Arthur and those who still
felt themselves as belonging to a Roman-British civilization
fought the invading Saxons to a standstill, and won a
temporary breathing-space. It didn't last, but it endured for a
generation or so, long enough for a whole world of legend to
be created round it, long enough to remain in folk-memory as
a Golden Age to which later people could look back with
longing and with wonder.

The Age of Arthur, as it has come down to us through the
poems and stories of the Middle Ages, is largely myth, but it
has a fabric of history. Because it is essentially British (or
Roman-British) history, and because the remnants of the
Roman-British were pushed back in the sixth century to the
fastnesses of Cornwall and Wales, much Arthurian history has
been transmitted through Celtic tales, the locations moving
westwards in the process, to Avalon, to Lyonesse and to
Gwynedd. Yet the historical campaign of the Roman-British
against the Saxons *must* have taken place nearer the Thames
— it makes no sense otherwise. The main Saxon raids of that
period were on the east and south-east coasts of England.
Once across the Thames in force the heart of southern
England lay open to them: their lines of communication east-
wards were secure, and without an Arthurian navy, of which
the legends give no hint, they could not be tackled at sea. But

if the Thames could be held by Arthurian troops the military picture becomes very different: the Saxons might control East Anglia, but the rich land south and west of the Thames, and the routes leading to the old centres of Roman-British prosperity in the south-west, would be denied to them. The Ridgeway forts command the Thames in its most sensitive area, where its upper reaches are narrow enough to be crossed without great difficulty. If the Saxons could be defeated here, and the river-line with its rearguard ring of hill-forts firmly held, then an Arthurian kingdom in the south-west would have a chance to develop. The reality of such history as can be discerned is in keeping with just such a situation: the king and his knights or chief captains vitally important to the survival of a kingdom that could be maintained only by vigilant defence. And with the death of the king, and the break-up of his 'Round Table' of knightly commanders, the disciplined vigilance would go, to be followed by fresh in-roads of invasion and the final collapse of the Arthurian realm. Something like this undoubtedly *did* happen, and the geographical setting for victory and ultimate defeat must have involved the line of Ridgeway forts, and the great Wansdyke constructed to support them.

The later King Alfred so dominates both history and legend of the Ridgeway countryside that it sometimes seems as if there were no history between the collapse of Roman power early in the fifth century and the rise of Alfred late in the ninth century. The four hundred and fifty years in between are Britain's Dark Ages, for which there are next to no historical sources, and not much archaeology — at least, not much that can be reckoned in any way decisive. The nearest historical writings — and they are not very near — are a record of the Saxon conquest of Britain* compiled in Wales about the middle of the sixth century (*c*.540-45) by a monk called Gildas, and Bede's *History of the English Church and People* which was written nearly two hundred years later, and which draws considerably on Gildas.

Yet tradition, although misty, cannot be ignored, and the

De Excidio et Conquestu Britanniae

126

tradition, recorded by both Gildas and Bede, asserts that after a period of confusion and savage Saxon raiding in the first half of the fifth century the Roman-British population rallied under a leader called Ambrosius Aurelianus and at the end of the century (*c.* 493-500) succeeded in defeating the the Saxons at Badon Hill *(Mons Badonicus)* and driving them off for at least a generation. That generation was the period of King Arthur, a relative of and successor to Ambrosius.

Tradition here is to some extent borne out by archaeology. A number of Saxon weapons of about the right period have been dredged up from the Thames near Wallingford, which is at least consistent with a hurried flight across the river by a routed army. And there are various earthworks which appear to be post-Roman roughly across the line of the Icknield Way in Buckinghamshire and Bedfordshire, which suggest a Saxon attempt to hold East Anglia — their main stronghold then — against attack from British forces in the west.

Tradition is also supported by the interesting place-name of Hinksey for what was originally an island in the Thames at Oxford, which made it possible to ford the river there — the original Oxen-ford. Hinksey means 'Hengist's island', and Hengist is reputed to have been the leader of the early Saxon invaders thrown out for a time by Ambrosius and Arthur.

It is impossible to do more than guess at dates. Jacquetta Hawkes is surely right in holding that the great earthwork called the Wansdyke could have been constructed only by a people organized under some strong military authority, and if the Wansdyke was built around the middle of the fifth century, it is reasonable to regard it as the work of Ambrosius, who rallied the British population. But this would make him rather old to command at Badon Hill. The story, however, is further complicated, or perhaps simplified, by the probability that there were two men called Ambrosius, father and son. If Ambrosius the Elder organized the Wansdyke defences, Ambrosius the Younger may have advanced to defeat the enemy at Badon. Or Arthur may have been in command by then.

Where was Badon Hill? It has been located all over Britain. One school of Arthurian scholarship places it near Bath.* This seems to me to ignore the strategical background to the campaign. The Saxons then had absolute superiority at sea and in rivers which their longboats could enter. They were soon in the Thames, and there is no reason to doubt that an early Saxon leader called Hengist installed himself at Oxford. The Roman-British counter-attack was prepared behind the Wansdyke and the line of Ridgeway forts. Bath is too far west: if the Saxons were in force at Bath the Roman-British defences had been turned. And if somehow the main Saxon force had been defeated near Bath the survivors would have had little hope of retreating across the Thames.

That strategical situation recurred precisely in King Alfred's campaign against the Danes. By then the Anglo-Saxons were settled farmers, and seapower had passed to the Vikings. They too, commanded the Thames, and Alfred's concern was to entice them away from the river and engage them on the Downs. His victory at Ashdown (in 870) was achieved in just such circumstances. The Danes held Reading, and sought to turn the flank of the Downs by advancing up the Kennet valley. Alfred and his brother Ethelred I *wanted* such an advance. They fell back towards the Downs, encouraging the Danish force to pursue. Then, at Ashdown, wherever that may have been, they stood at bay. Perhaps they drew reserves from the Ridgeway forts. At any rate they won, and gave the Danes a sharp lesson; they also gave themselves a useful lesson, proving that the Danes, once away from their boats, could be beaten.

Five centuries earlier the Saxons were in the position of the Danes. They could come to the east coast as they pleased, they commanded the Thames estuary and the Upper Thames. Ambrosius (or Arthur) held the Ridgeway forts. The tactical need was the same — to provoke an advance from the Thames, and fight on the Downs.

We have at least some contemporary record of the Battle of

*John Morris, The Age of Arthur (Weidenfeld & Nicolson, London, 1973)

Ashdown, hard as it may now be to interpret: the engagement is described by King Alfred's biographer, Asser. We have nothing remotely contemporary about Badon, except that tradition maintains that the battle lasted for three days. But there *is* a place actually called Baydon near the Ridgeway, with just the right sort of high ground for such an encounter. If the name of Badon Hill is accepted for the battle — as it must be — is it not likely that the hill was in fact at Baydon? This Baydon is on a spur of high ground two and a half miles south of the fort called Alfred's Castle, the intermediate or supporting hill-fort between Liddington and Uffington. The Baydon ridge is high, rising to 240 metres (787 feet), and it commands the valley of the upper Lambourn and a wide stretch of sensitive countryside *within* the line of Ridgeway forts. The Roman road from Cirencester to Newbury runs across the Baydon ridge, and this road crosses the Ridgeway at Foxhill.

282780

277822

If we assume, as I think we can, that Ambrosius or Arthur held the Ridgeway forts, the Saxons, if they were to break out from the Thames, needed to capture or to turn the forts. They are formidable to attack from the north, but they could be turned from the south, if a sufficient force could be got there. The valley of the Lambourn, which runs into the Kennet at Newbury, offers the best route for doing this. The Danes, in similar circumstances, were trying to advance up the Kennet valley before Alfred and his brother defeated them at Ashdown. The Saxons, five hundred years earlier, may have tried to strike into the heart of the Roman-British defences in exactly the same way — up the Kennet valley to Newbury, and then up the Lambourn valley to take the Ridgeway fortresses from the rear.

The Roman-British commander, Ambrosius the Younger, or Arthur, if he had succeeded to the command by then, may have invited the Saxons to do just this, as Alfred and his brother invited the Danes to pursue them to the Downs. Whether we call him Ambrosius or Arthur, the Roman-British commander was trained in the Roman tradition: he understood the use of roads, and he knew the Roman road across the Downs. If he could entice the Saxon host into the Lambourn valley he could make his stand on Baydon ridge, and bring up reinforcements quickly by the Roman road.

This is not guesswork; it is simply an appreciation of the military situation dictated by the physical features of the land, the same now as they were in Arthur's day. Whether the Roman-British commander did entice the Saxons into his trap at Baydon we cannot say; what we can say is that such an exploitation of a military situation would have appealed to an able commander of any age; indeed it was successfully practised by King Alfred in similar circumstances later.

Given a Saxon defeat at Baydon, the rest of the picture falls into place — the flight to the Thames through the marshes of the Vale of the White Horse, the desperate haste of those who reached the Thames to cross the river, throwing away weapons in order to swim for it. The tradition of a battle that went on for three days is also explained. The Saxons were not merely defeated, they were routed; and as groups of their broken army tried to flee from the Downs into the vale they were harried and cut to pieces by Roman-British detachments coming after them from the Ridgeway. There is some evidence to support such running fights, for a group of skeletons turned up by the plough on the slopes of Whitehorse Hill seem to have been buried hastily, more or less where they fell, as might be expected when victorious pursuers had little time for funerals. Some had objects near them that appear to be Saxon, others were apparently of Roman-British origin, so the period seems approximately right.

It remains to be asked, was the village of Baydon called Baydon as far back as the end of the fifth century? It is an uncommon name; there is no other place in England called by it. Ekwall, in his great *Dictionary of English Place-Names*, has a medieval reference to it in the Salisbury Charters in a Latin form as *Beidona* and he derives it from the Old English '*Beg-dun*', meaning a down or hill once noted for the berries to be gathered there. The description is apt enough for any sheltered slope. The broken Saxons, cut off from whatever

Bailey Hill near Baydon

supplies they had, may have had to eat berries as they fled: it is the kind of thing that would live on in folk-memory, and they may have caled the encounter the Battle of the Hill of the Wild Berries. Gildas, writing half a century later, when the Saxons had come back and were completing their conquest of England, may well have Latinized the Old English name into *Mons Badonicus*, and Bede followed him. The name as well as the place seems to fit the period.

I have wondered, too, whether some of the many Alfred legends of the Ridgeway countryside do not more properly belong to Arthur's time: the magical Blowing Stone, for example; so with Alfred's Castle — should it, perhaps, be Arthur's Castle, a key point in the fighting round Badon Hill? Certainly the Roman-British victory at Badon Hill was real, wherever it may have been won. If, as I think, the Ridgeway and its forts helped to determine that victory, it would be in keeping with its ancient purpose of defending a civilization. I like to think of them providing a secure frontier for Arthur's kingdom, while he lived and gave men a will to defend it.

The physical diversion to Baydon is best — and most appropriately — made by the Roman road (marked on the Ordnance Survey map as such) that runs dead straight south-east from the inn at Foxhill. It then goes more nearly east, turns slightly south and continues arrow-straight up the steep escarpment to Baydon village — a total of four miles. There are superb views as the road climbs and you can feel that you are following the march of Roman-British soldiers brought hurriedly from Liddington early one autumn morning at the end of the fifth century to reinforce the men holding the high ground at Baydon and to inflict a decisive defeat on the Saxons. The Roman road to Baydon is defended to the north by a strong-point of the fort now known as Alfred's Castle. A mile to the east of Baydon village, on high ground dominating the upper Lambourn valley, are the remains of an interesting ditch or earthwork, which at least fits the theory that this was the ground chosen by Ambroisus or Arthur for the battle that established Arthur's kingdom.

232813

277822

293783

131

Map D: Foxhill to Blowingstone Hill

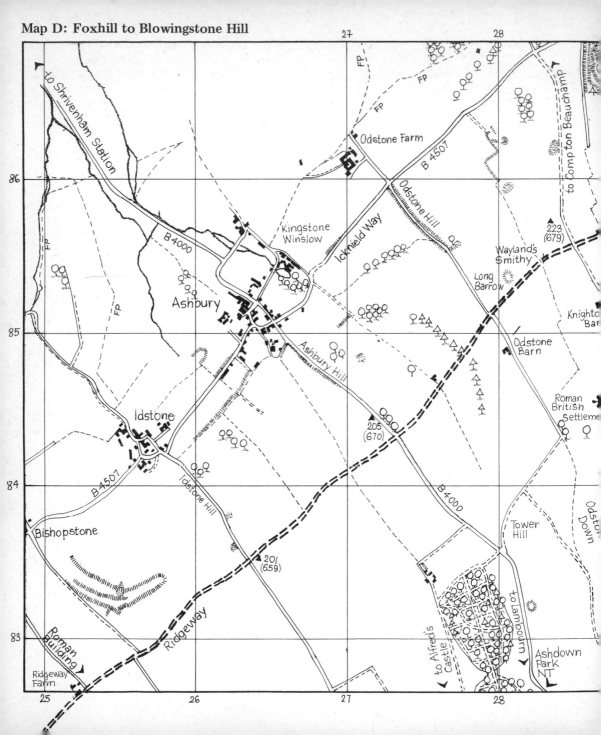

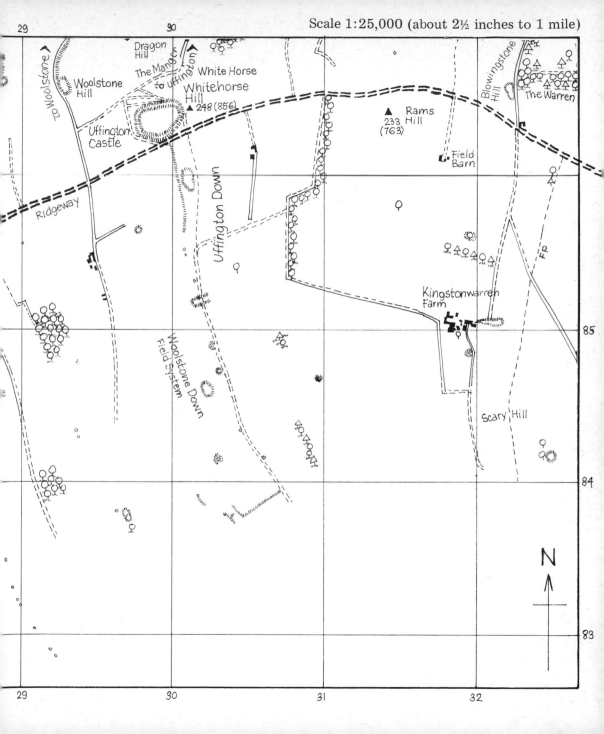

Scale 1:25,000 (about 2½ inches to 1 mile)

6 Whitehorse Downs

Strip lynchets near Bishopstone.

233814

244822

244825

On leaving the Shepherd's Rest a walk of about a hundred
yards along the Bishopstone road brings you again to the
unmetalled Ridgeway: the metalled road goes northwards to
get to Bishopstone via Hinton Parva, the Ridgeway runs north-
east. On leaving the metalled road one is back at once in
Ridgeway country. The path runs through a beech coppice,
and immediately begins to climb the southern shoulder of
Charlbury Hill. When the trees of the little coppice fall away,
there is a great sweep of open country on both flanks and
ahead. About a mile on, after climbing the shoulder of
Charlbury Hill and descending to a little valley between the
hill to the north and Lammy Down to the south, a track
crosses the Ridgeway, running from south-west to north-
west. A diversion of about a quarter of a mile along the
north-west arm will take you to a splendid little group of
prehistoric terraced fields, marked on the map as 'strip
lynchets'. These terraces or 'lynchets' are a typical feature of
the White Horse Downs which you are now approaching;
from a little distance they can look like a giant staircase
climbing up a hillside. Some of them are perhaps natural,
caused by rain and weathering of the chalk, but others are
certainly man-made, the hillside cut back and field surfaces
laboriously built up to provide an area for growing crops on
land that is otherwise too steep to till. This group of terraces,
though on a smaller scale, is as perfect as anything to be seen
on a Mediterranean hillside, where peasant industry over
the centuries has terraced steep surfaces for vines or olive
groves. The site is well chosen, on the side of a sheltered
coombe once cut and smoothed by ice, and the little fields
face east and south, to make the most of the sun. What was

grown there three or four thousand years ago one cannot know — barley probably, wheat perhaps. Maybe our distant forbears fermented some of their barley to make beer. Their hard work certainly deserved it.

Returning from the lynchets to the Ridgeway, another mile takes the track to Ridgeway Farm — from digging-stick to tractor, man has farmed over this same land from the begin-

ning of human settlement. And the land has provided more than sustenance — it has given wealth. Less than a mile to the south-east of the present Ridgeway Farm is the site of a 259816 Roman building, where some substantial citizen of the second or third century A.D. had his villa. And a mile and a half east of the Roman site is the grand gentleman's residence of 283820 Ashdown Park, built about 1660 for the first Earl of Craven. On Swinley Down, just to the west of Ashdown Park, is a 277822 now-somewhat-flattened hill-fort known as Alfred's Castle. This is a much smaller earthwork than the great fortresses of Barbury, Liddington and Uffington, but it seems part of the same strategic plan: it lies about a mile south of the Ridgeway, roughly halfway between Liddington and Uffington, and could have been a strong-point to assist in keeping open the lines of communication between the major forts. It also guards the Roman road to Baydon from the north, the significance of which has been discussed in the previous chapter.

The bank of Alfred's Castle was once strengthened by sarsens, some of which, following tradition in these matters, were broken up in the seventeenth century to provide building stone for Ashdown Park.

Ashdown Park

The house at Ashdown Park is a peculiarly attractive stately home, emphasizing the eccentricity of the British landed gentry as well as their (usually) good taste. It looks narrow for its height, and this is part of its attraction: Sir Nikolaus Pevsner has described it as 'the perfect doll's house'. It is a splendid phrase, for that is exactly what it is — a doll's house magnified to human scale (perhaps slightly superhuman, as befitting the earl for whom it was built). There is a pleasing sense of continuity in meeting this fine stately home in the same countryside where a retired Roman general, or prosperous Roman-British landowner, had his villa, though the villa, alas, has disappeared.

253827
246837

259833

At the Ridgeway Farm crossways a surfaced road leads off to Bishopstone (one mile further on) a pretty village with a nice duck pond. Just beyond Bishopstone the Ridgeway crosses the county boundary for Wiltshire into what used to be Berkshire, but became part of the enlarged county of Oxfordshire on April 1st, 1974. Whether old Berkshire or new Oxfordshire is irrelevant to the landscape, but there are subtle differences in the texture of the countryside on leaving Wiltshire. The Downs become rounder and a little softer, and there are fewer scattered sarsens. Marlborough and Avebury belong to the Kennet; in the Vale of the White Horse you begin to sense the Thames. I have always thought, and think still, that the turf of the White Horse Downs (the old Berkshire Downs) is smoother and more springy than the turf of the Wiltshire Downs. However this may be, the Ridgeway strides on, true to its ancient character in running near the crest of the Downs, keeping above the spring-line and commanding extensive views over the valleys.

273843

Crossing the Ashbury-Lambourn road at a height of some 205 metres (672 feet), the track enters perhaps its most famous stretch. In just over three miles it passes the magnificent

281854   Megalithic tomb known as 'Wayland's Smithy'; Uffington
298864, 298869   Castle and Whitehorse Hill; Dragon Hill, on which St George
324872   is reputed to have slain his dragon; and the Blowing Stone,
which King Alfred is said to have blown in order to rally his
men in some fierce battle against the Danes.

281854   Wayland's Smithy comes first, about a mile after the main
road. It stands in a little wood, about fifty yards off the
Ridgeway, on a commanding bluff that in some qualities of
light seems to be almost in the sky. Its Saxon name embodies

Wayland's Smithy

a local legend that if you leave your horse by the tomb, with a coin on the lintel stone, you can return to find it shod by Wayland, the smith of the old Saxon gods. But the tomb was there two thousand years before Saxon gods were heard of on the Ridgeway. It is a very early Megalithic long barrow, older even than the West Kennett Long Barrow, going back, per-haps, to about 2800 B.C. Like the West Kennett barrow, it served as a mausoleum for centuries, the home in death of members of a dynasty which, one may suppose, ruled over a great sweep of this land a thousand years before the Greeks had heard of Troy. The tomb, built of sarsens and entered between imposing sarsen pillars, belongs to the same culture as the West Kennett barrow, showing that much the same sort of social organization existed at this end of the Downs as around Avebury.

The Ridgeway between Wayland's Smithy and Uffington Hill

The Ridgeway is often banked, or slightly banked, along its edges, and the banks are sometimes planted with rather

straggling hedges: it is high country for hedgerows, and the winds keep them sparse. On this stretch the hedges are more thickset, so that the route by Wayland's Smithy has something of the air of a ceremonial avenue. (The path, though, is much rutted, and is muddy and slippery after rain.) A mile beyond the Smithy it runs by the great bank of Uffington Castle, which dominates the Vale from the summit of Whitehorse Hill (261 metres, 858 feet). The castle, or fort, encloses

300863

Dragon Hill and
Uffington Horse

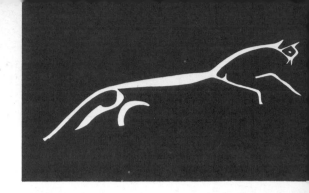

Diagram and detailed
abstracts of the White Horse

143

The Manger from Whitehorse
Hill

Uffington Church

Thatch at Woolstone

eight and a half acres, and the bank and ditch are still steep. There is almost always a wind here, and the bold, treeless ramparts, where you can walk or run easily, make one of the finest sites in England for flying kites. On the hillside that makes the northern flank of the hill is cut the most famous of hill-figures in Europe, the long White Horse of Uffington (the village in the valley below). You can walk up to it (but not, please, on its chalk outlines) but you cannot see it very well from the hill itself, because you are too close. The horse can be better seen from a mile or so off on the Swindon-Wantage road (B4507), and better still from a train on the old Great Western main line (now British Rail's Western Region) that runs through the Vale some two and a half miles away. The horse is a magnificent creature, nearly 110 metres (360 feet) long by 48.5 metres (160 feet) high, slender and beautifully proportioned, and seeming to be galloping uphill. The lines and perspective are perfect — how its unknown artist scaled so accurately a figure that can only be seen whole at a distance of about a mile is not the least of the mysteries of this mysterious horse. More moving still, perhaps, is to envisage the mind of the unknown artist as he sculpted his horse. All he could see as he worked was a series of detailed abstract shapes — an eye, a hoof, a fetlock: parts in the end of a coherent and beautiful whole, but, as he worked, incidents, merely, of an artist's vision. It is one of the more wonderful manifestations of the mind of man.

Hardly anything at all is known about it. Because the area is believed to have formed part of the territory of a non-Belgic tribe called the Dobunni in the first century A.D., and because a silver coin of the Dobunni with an emblem of a horse was found in Uffington Castle, it is assumed that the horse was their tribal emblem, and was cut on the hillside around the first century A.D. — an official plate put up by the Ministry of Works (Department of the Environment) which is now responsible for the figure duly tells you so. The evidence is thin. A line of chalk cannot be dated (except to the cretaceous seas that formed it in the geological past millions of years ago). The White Horse may be one thousand or two thousand years older than the notice suggests. It may conceivably, be younger — local tradition, which attributes everything in these parts to King Alfred, who was born at Wantage, has it that the horse was cut to commemorate one of Alfred's victories over the Danes. Lacking a historian of any sort, the White Horse must be left to excite wonder at the skill of its artist in the distant past.

Across a steep coombe ('The Manger') to the north-west of the horse is a curious flat-topped hill, slightly resembling Silbury Hill, though it is assumed to be natural. This is Dragon Hill, on which, so tradition has it, St George fought and slew his dragon. It is a splendid site for dragon-slaying, and on-lookers could have had safe ringside-seats on the slopes of Whitehorse Hill.

298869

Compton Beauchamp Church

A diversion (by surfaced roads) to Uffington two and a half miles away is rewarding. It is an attractive village, with facilities in the way of inns, and a remarkable eight-sided church tower. Thomas Hughes, who wrote *Tom Brown's Schooldays*, was born at Uffington in 1822 and spent his early boyhood there. The opening chapters of *Tom Brown* have some fine descriptions of the White Horse and its countryside, though the history (much of it about Alfred) is a little fanciful. Further diversions to the neighbouring villages of Woolstone (one and a half miles) and Compton Beauchamp (one mile on from Woolstone) are equally rewarding — Woolstone for the lovely thatch of its cottages, Compton Beauchamp for its beautiful little chalk church and gentle, hidden churchyard. In the churchyard is the grave of a child who died in infancy in the eighteenth century. The lettering can still be made out:

294877
283871

> *When the Archangel's trump shall blow*
> *And soul and body join,*
> *What crowds shall wish their life below*
> *Had been as brief as thine.*

324864

From Whitehorse Hill the Ridgeway descends a little (but not much) to pass the shoulder of Rams Hill and cross the metalled road from Uffington and Kingston Lisle to Lambourn

on Blowingstone Hill. Rams Hill (233 metres, 764 feet) has another hill-fort, surrounding the much older enclosure dated to about 1500 B.C. (already mentioned, see p. 102). The fort is not nearly so formidable as Uffington Castle, and, like Alfred's Castle and other minor fortifications, was presumably a supporting strong-point for the line of major fortresses.

324872

A walk of just over half a mile down Blowingstone Hill towards Kingston Lisle takes you to the Blowing Stone. It stands under a tree in the garden of a cottage that in 'Tom Brown's' days was an inn. The stone is a block of sarsen riddled with curious natural holes, like a great block of Gruyère cheese. By blowing into one of the holes the stone can be made to emit a sort of deep trumpet-note. Naturally, King Alfred is supposed to have used it in one of his battles, though it would seem to fit Arthurian legend better.

Distances from Foxhill to Blowingstone Hill	
Foxhill to Ashbury-Lambourn road (B4000)	3¼ miles
Diversion to strip lynchets	½ mile
Diversion into Bishopstone and return to Ridgeway	1½ miles
Diversion to Alfred's Castle and return	2½ miles
B4000 crossing to Wayland's Smithy	1 mile
Perambulation of Uffington Castle and on Whitehorse Hill	1 mile
Whitehorse Hill to Blowingstone Hill	1¼ miles
Diversion to Blowing Stone and back	1 mile
Diversion to Uffington and return to Ridgeway	5 miles
Round trip Whitehorse Hill-Uffington-Woolstone-Compton Beauchamp and return to Ridgeway	7 miles
Total Ridgeway walk without diversions	6¼ miles

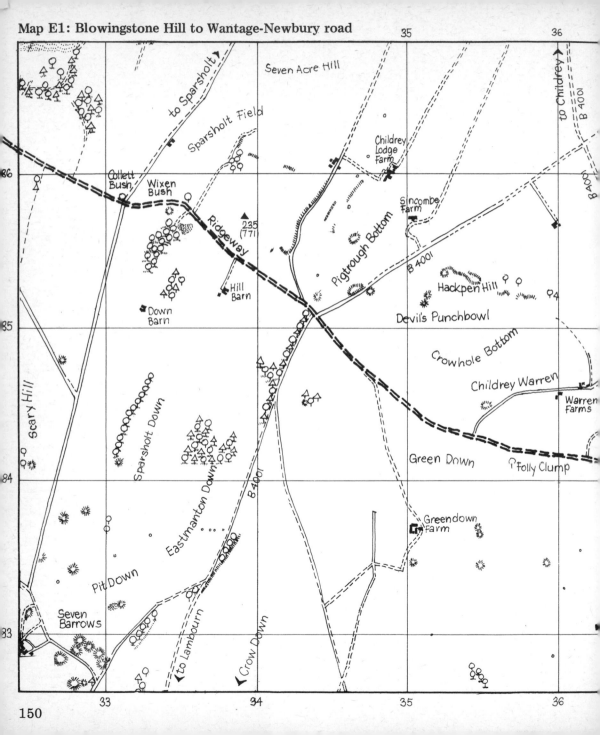

to Sparsholt

Seven Acre Hill

to Childrey

B 4001

Sparsholt Field

Childrey
Lodge
Farm

Collett
Bush

Wixen
Bush

Ridgeway

235
(771)

Sincombe
Farm

Pigtrough Bottom

B 4001

Hackpen Hill

Hill
Barn

Down
Barn

Devil's Punchbowl

Crowhole Bottom

Scary Hill

Childrey Warren

Warren
Farms

Sparsholt Down

Eastmanton Down

B 4001

Green Down

Folly Clump

Greendown
Farm

Pit Down

Seven
Barrows

to Lambourn

Crow Down

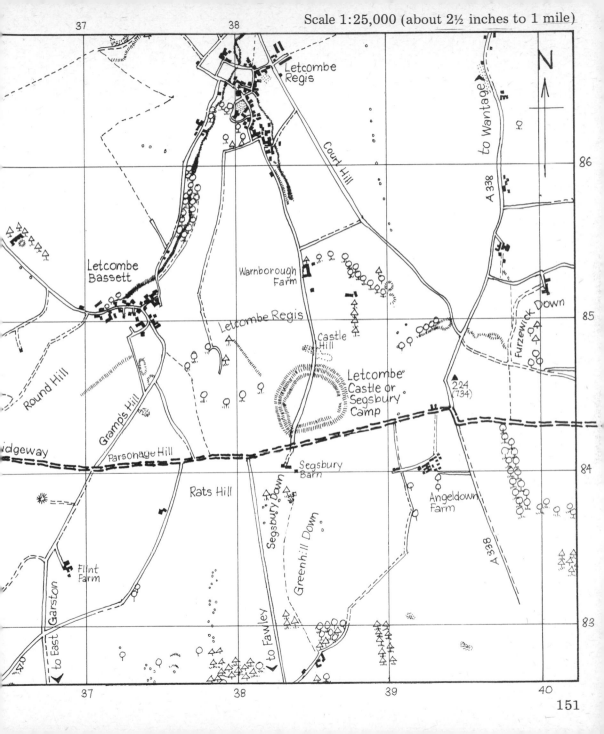

Scale 1:25,000 (about 2½ inches to 1 mile)

N

37   38

Letcombe
Regis

to Wantage

A 338

Court Hill

86

Letcombe
Bassett

Warnborough
Farm

Letcombe Regis

Furzewick Down

85

Castle
Hill

Round Hill

Letcombe
Castle or
Segsbury
Camp

224
(734)

Gramps Hill

Ridgeway

Parsonage Hill

Segsbury
Barn

84

Rats Hill

Segsbury Down

Angeldown
Farm

A 338

Flint
Farm

Greenhill Down

to East Garston

to Fawley

83

37   38   39   40

151

Map E2: Wantage-Newbury road to Schutchamer Knob

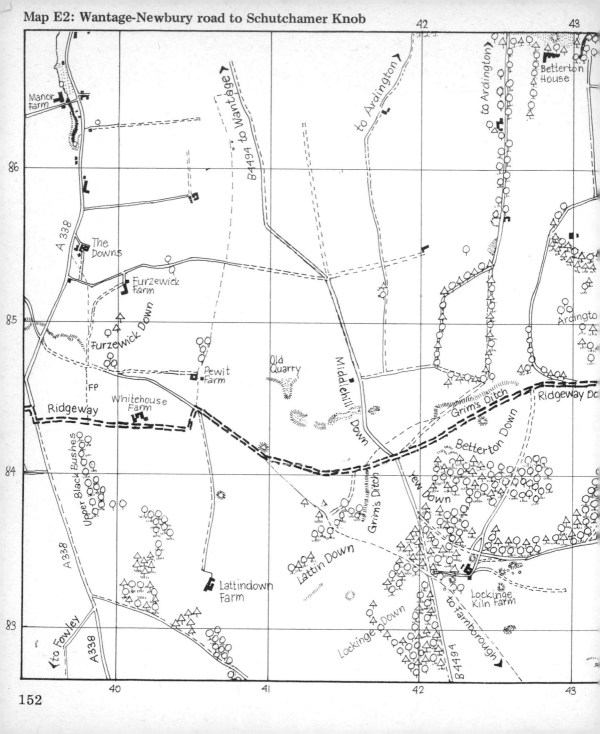

Manor Farm

A 338

The Downs

Furzewick Farm

Furzewick Down

FP

Ridgeway

Whitehouse Farm

Pewit Farm

Old Quarry

Middlehill Down

B 4494 to Wantage

to Ardington

to Ardington

Betterton House

Ardingto

Grim's Ditch

Ridgeway Do

Betterton Down

Upper Black Bushes

Grim's Ditch

Yew Down

A 338

Lattin Down

Lattin Down

Lattindown Farm

Lockinge Down

Lockinge Kiln Farm

to Farnborough

to Fawley

A 338

B 4494

42

43

86

85

84

83

40

41

42

43

152

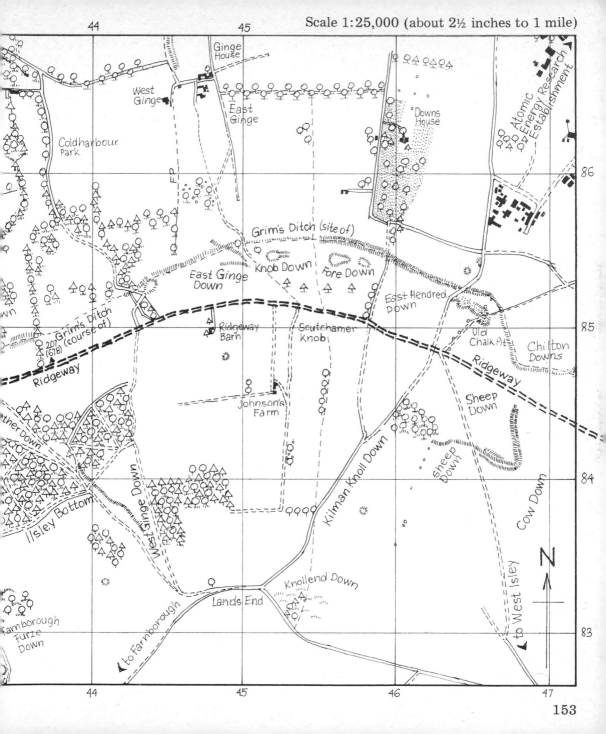

44   45

Ginge House

West Ginge

East Ginge

Coldharbour Park

Downs House

Atomic Energy Research Establishment

FP

86

Grim's Ditch (site of)

Knob Down   Fore Down

East Ginge Down

East Hendred Down

Grim's Ditch (course of)

207 (618)

Ridgeway Barn

Scutchamer Knob

Old Chalk Pit

Chilton Downs

85

Ridgeway

Ridgeway

Johnson's Farm

Sheep Down

ther Down

Sheep Down

Kilman Knoll Down

84

Ilsley Bottom

West Ginge Down

Cow Down

to West Isley

N

Knollend Down

Farnborough Furze Down

Lands End

to Farnborough

83

44   45   46   47

7 The Best Turf in the World

Old flint workings above the Devil's Punchbowl

Across Blowingstone Hill the Ridgeway climbs again in the next mile from 205 metres (674 feet) to 242 metres (793 feet). This is a lovely stretch, stiff walking on much-rutted chalk, but you gain height steadily, and to the north open up ever more splendid views over the middle reaches of the Vale of the White Horse. At the top of the climb the Ridgeway meets a minor road running downhill to Sparsholt (a nice little village, with a pub, a mile and a half away) and then the main road (B4001) from Wantage to Lambourn.

332858

346876
344851

A diversion of about a mile along the road towards Lambourn and a walk of about half a mile over Pit Down (turning at map reference 336834) brings you to a remarkable group of Bronze Age tombs known as Seven Barrows. Actually there are (or were, for over the centuries some have been levelled by the plough) at least twenty-six barrows, mostly the more or less standard bell-shaped barrow used over the graves of men, but also some of the 'disc' and 'saucer' barrows that seem usually to have been erected over women's graves. A little to the north of the group of Bronze Age Beaker burials is a chambered Long Barrow belonging to their Neolithic predecessors, a moving testimony to the long sanctity of a burial ground. The place still inspires awe, though without the grandeur of the great dynastic tombs at Wayland's Smithy and West Kennett, but nearer, somehow, to common humanity — the final resting place of men and women who walked this same stretch of countryside, who lived and loved and worried about tomorrow three to five thousand years ago.

329829

Back on the summit of Sparsholt Down the Ridgeway carries

347847 on across the main road to skirt Childrey Warren and a huge rolling dip in the Downs known as the Devil's Punchbowl. The Ridgeway is fenced here, for there are training-gallops for racehorses nearby, but an exceptionally high stile, apparently made for giants (or, perhaps, the Devil) leads to a path that runs by the rim of the Punchbowl. The turf here is, to my thinking, the finest on the Downs, which is to say the best turf in the world, not grass merely but an intricate texture of fine grass and the tiny heads of wild flowers, each with its cushion of little leaves. With an immense sky above you, and the great dip of the Punchbowl falling away below, you feel that you are walking on air.

353853 To the north of the Punchbowl there is a hillock or tumulus (marked on the map) and beyond the tumulus there is an area of curiously broken ground, like the remains of quarrying on a doll's house scale, which I think must once have been open-cast flint workings, though they are not marked as such. Where the chalk is exposed there are plenty of flint-cores still to be seen, and you can re-create in your imagination a vivid picture of prehistoric men working away with antler-picks to get at them. The little pits of these old workings have another interesting effect — they illustrate the remarkable differences in micro-climates over a few square yards of the same area. In spring you can see cowslips sheltered by one of the pit banks flowering on normal-sized stalks of two or three inches, whereas on the exposed top of the bank they remain miniature cowslips, flowering almost directly from the ground. There are similar differences in other flora. In spite of myxomatosis, there are nearly always rabbits to be seen in Childrey Warren; it is a comforting example (in one sense, for the rabbit is not wholly a friend to man) of the survival of a species through the deadliest of plagues. The warren, a honeycomb of burrows, is on the lower slopes to one side of the dip, towards the floor or bottom of the Punchbowl. To the east, the bowl rises so smoothly that you get a sense of the hillside flowing into it. Aeons ago it was smoothed by ice, and you can almost see the glacier curling over the rim of the hill to carve out the sweet high valley where the spring-line now is, just above Letcombe Bassett.

The Letcombes — Bassett and Regis — are worth a diversion. The best route is by way of Gramp's Hill, where a track going north and south crosses the Ridgeway about a mile and a quarter on from the stile leading to the Punchbowl. Letcombe Bassett is three quarters of a mile downhill, along the north-going track. Letcombe Regis, the bigger of the two villages, is a mile farther on downhill. The springs form a rivulet to flow through the village, the Letcombe Brook. Its water is exqui-sitely clear, and it has long been famous for growing water-cress — 'Bassett Cress!' was one of the street cries of early nineteenth-century London. For such a minute village Letcombe Bassett has a rather grand place in literature. It is the Cresscombe of *Jude the Obscure*, which Thomas Hardy wrote there, and Jonathan Swift spent his last summer in England (1714) at Letcombe Bassett Rectory before going off to Ireland. At Letcombe he wrote his 'Verses on Himself', and there he was visited by Alexander Pope. Letcombe Regis has rather more in the way of amenities, if less of a place in literature. It also has some particularly fine thatch.

A mile on from the Gramp's Hill crossways is Segsbury Down, where we find the next of the Ridgeway's major fortresses, called variously Letcombe Castle or Segsbury Camp. At 209 metres (687 feet) this massive hill-fort, enclosing some twenty-six acres, dominates Wantage and the Vale northwards to Oxford, and, particularly, the network of valley tracks (now main roads) that meet and cross in Wantage. The Cirencester-Reading road (A417) and the Oxford-Andover road (A338) intersect here. Both have been important routes from anti-

372841

374852
382865

385845

The Devil's Punchbowl

quity, being tracks of firm ground providing passage across
the once densely wooded and treacherously marshy Vale of
the White Horse. The Vale is the wide valley of the river Ock,
which rises near Uffington and flows sluggishly through the
relatively low-lying valley to join the Thames at Abingdon. It
has numerous small tributaries, even today still liable to flood
and the marshy nature of the valley is shown by the 'ey'
ending (old English for 'island'), in many of its place-names —
Charney, Goosey, East and West Hanney and Pusey among
them. The fortress on Segsbury Down is well sited to
command all the crossings of the marsh.

As in a number of the other Ridgeway forts, the earthworks

at Segsbury were once reinforced with sarsens. The bank is still impressive, and with the ground in front of it falling away steeply, the fort would still be a formidable place to attack without artillery. What battles were once fought there, and what sallies made from it, no one knows. It is dreamily quiet now, and its bank is a grand place to sit on a clear day, looking north-east towards the Thames some twelve miles away. On a bright day in winter you may get a glint of the river, but at most times of the year it is hidden by its willows. You can make out the line of the river from its trees.

398880   If you need the amenities of a town, Wantage is a good place. It has most facilities: shops, inns, taxis, doctors, a hospital, and a fine old market square adorned with a large (Victorian) statue of King Alfred, who was born at Wantage in A.D. 849. He had a palace in or near the town, but it was probably made of wood, and nothing remains to show where it was. Local
394883   tradition places it on a hill at Belmont, about half a mile to the north-west of the present town centre. (To save a rather dull main-road walk into Wantage, you could telephone for a taxi from Letcombe Regis, which is only about a mile and a half outside the town.)

417842   From Segsbury Down the Ridgeway winds on to cross the Wantage-Newbury road (B4494) some two and a half miles south-east of Wantage, and after crossing the road enters a stretch of Downland peculiarly rich in sections of prehistoric ditches. They run mostly near the Ridgeway, a few hundred yards to the north of it and roughly parallel with its track. No one knows their purpose. They are called generically 'Grim's Ditch', which suggests that they are pre-Saxon, for 'Grim' was another name for Woden, and when the Saxons didn't know who made something they were inclined to put it down to Woden. These earthworks may be defensive: their position protecting the Ridgeway from the north is in keeping with the strategical thinking behind the line of fortresses. But it has also been suggested that they formed tribal boundaries.

The Ridgeway here runs near the 200-metre (656-foot)

contour, the Downs gradually falling towards the Thames,
but still high above the surrounding countryside. To the
north the land falls more steeply to the Vale, and on the
lower slopes, between two and three miles away from the old,
high track, a line of beautiful small villages grew up where
there was water. These villages, Ardington, West Hendred,
East Hendred and Harwell are strung out along the lower
route, the Icknield Way, that became more convenient for

Left Water-cress ponds at
Letcombe Bassett
Below left Segsbury Castle
Below East Hendred Church

travellers as the land was settled and there was less danger
from wild animals, and from men to whom every stranger
was liable to be taken for an enemy.

The Ginge Brook, which flows between the two Hendreds
(they are less than a mile apart) brought substantial prosperity
to these villages in late medieval times. It had a forceful
enough flow to power water-mills, not only to grind corn but
also to work fulling-mills for beating and 'fulling' the cloth
which was once made in the district. The brook was also
useful for retting flax (soaking it, to make the fibres soft
enough to spin), and the villages had a valuable trade in both
linen and wool. The past survives on the modern map. A hill
on the Ridgeway, at the top of East Ginge Down, is still
called 'Scutchamer Knob' — a 'scutcher' was a man who beat
out (scutched) the retted flax. Scutchamer Knob was the
villagers' place for festivities, and people would come for
miles to attend a fair there.

Distances from Blowingstone Hill to Scutchamer Knob	
Blowingstone Hill to Sparsholt summit	1½ miles
Diversion to Sparsholt (for a drink?) and return	3 miles
Diversion to Lambourn Seven Barrows and return	3 miles
Sparsholt summit to Devil's Punchbowl stile	½ mile
Walk round Punchbowl and return	2½ miles
Devil's Punchbowl stile to Gramp's Hill	1½ miles
Diversion to the Letcombes and return	3½ miles
Gramp's Hill to Segsbury Fort	1 mile
Segsbury Fort to Wantage-Newbury road (B4494)	2 miles
B4494 crossing to Scutchamer Knob	2½ miles
Total Ridgeway walk without diversions	9 miles
Visit to Wantage — add 4 miles	

Atomic Energy
Research
Establishment
Harwell

to Harwell

A 34

course of old railway

85

Old Chalk Pit

Chilton Downs

Grim's Ditch

Ridge Hill

Ridgeway

Old Chalk Pit

Bury Down

Kate's Gore

84

Cow Down

Sheep Down

FP

Bury Down

Folly Down

184 (587)

Sev

Gore Hill

Folly Barn

83

Hodcott Down

Abingdon Lane Down

Sheep Down

West Ilsley

FP

Boundary Mounds

82

Hodcott Farm

A 34

to East Ilsley

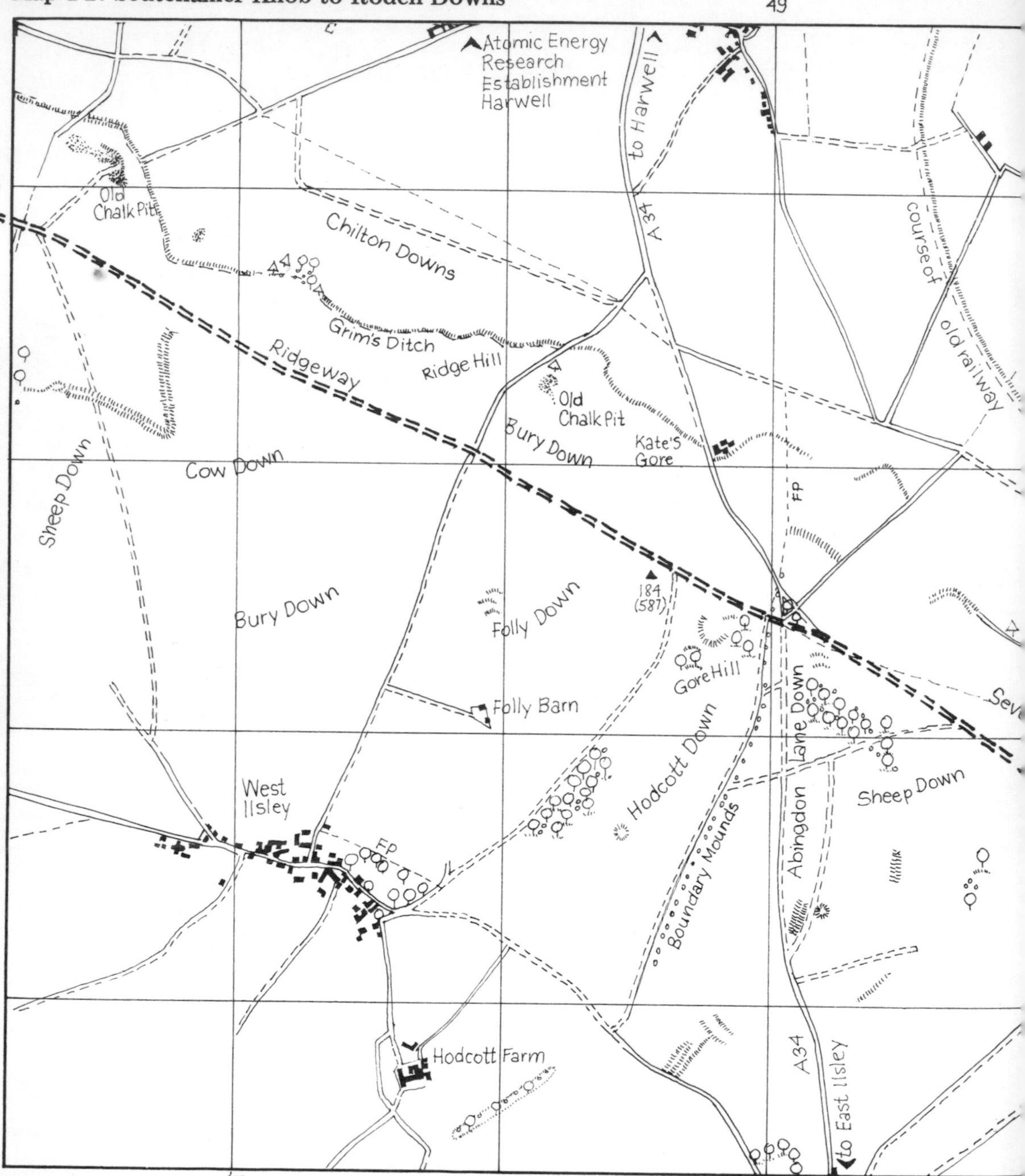

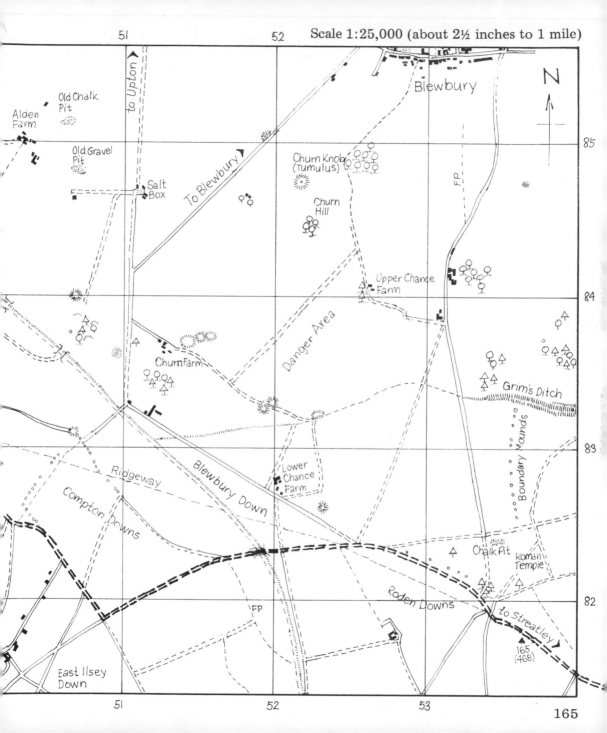

51 52

N

Blewbury

Old Chalk
Pit

Alden
Farm

To Upton

Old Gravel
Pit

To Blewbury

Salt
Box

Churn Knob
(Tumulus)

FP

Churn
Hill

85

Upper Chance
Farm

84

Churn Farm

Danger Area

Grim's Ditch

Boundary Mounds

83

Ridgeway

Blewbury Down

Lower
Chance
Farm

Compton Downs

Chalk Pit

Roman
Temple

Roden Downs

to Streatley

82

FP

East Ilsey
Down

165
(468)

51 52 53

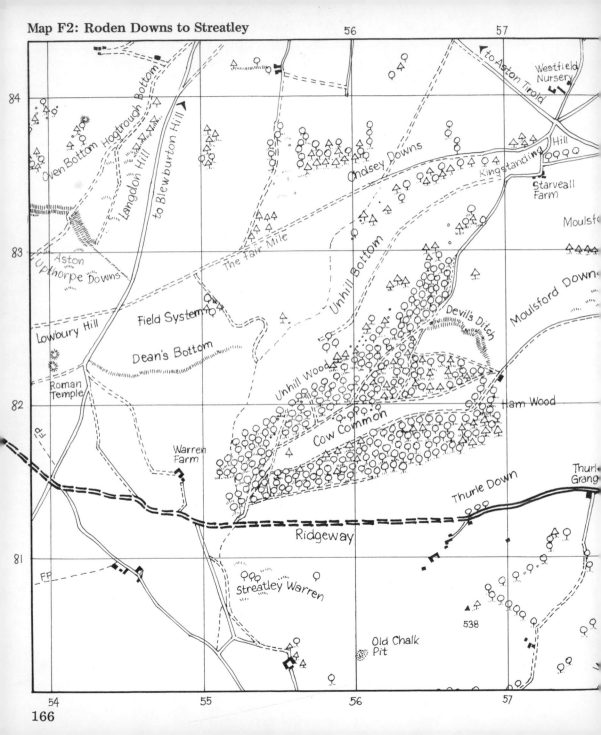

Map F2: Roden Downs to Streatley

Oven Bottom

Hogtrough Bottom

Langdon Hill

to Blewburton Hill

Cholsey Downs

to Aston Tirold

Westfield Nursery

Kingstanding Hill

Starveall Farm

Moulsf

Aston Upthorpe Downs

The Fair Mile

Unhill Bottom

Devil's Ditch

Moulsford Down

Lowbury Hill

Field System

Dean's Bottom

Unhill Wood

Moulsford Downs

Roman Temple

Cow Common

Ham Wood

Warren Farm

Thurle Down

Thurl Grang

Ridgeway

FP

Streatley Warren

538

Old Chalk Pit

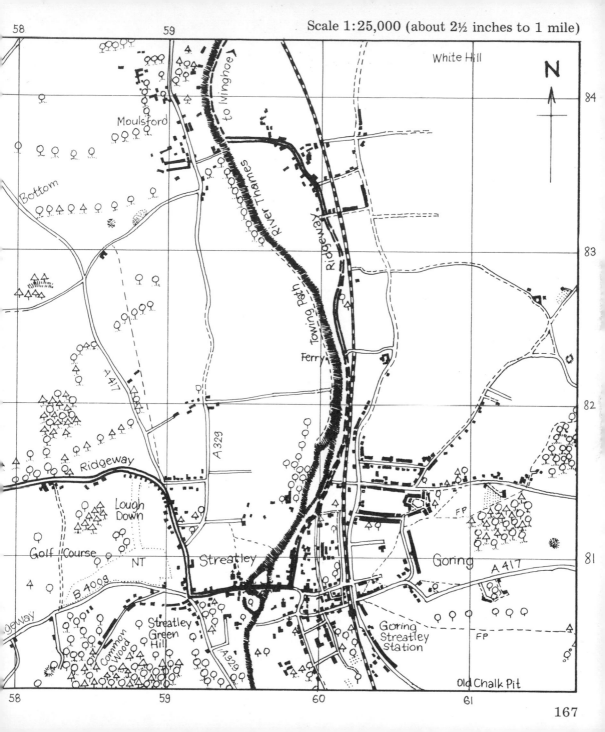

White Hill

N

84

Moulsford

Bottom

to Ivinghoe

River Thames

Towing Path

Ridgeway

83

Ferry

82

A 417

A 329

Ridgeway

Lough
Down

Golf Course

NT

Streatley

Goring

A 417

81

B 4009

Streatley
Green
Hill

Common Wood

A 329

Goring
Streatley
Station

FP

FP

Old Chalk Pit

Ridgeway

8　To the Thames

The Ridgeway skirts Ham
Wood (skyline, left) before
dipping down to the Thames

463848
485858

After Scutchamer Knob (at 202 metres, 664 feet) the Ridgeway although undulating with the rise and fall of the land,
begins to trend downhill towards the Thames. At East
Hendred Down (187 metres, 612 feet) you must pay attention
to navigation. A rather imposing track, looking much like the
Ridgeway, runs off north-east, but although this does take
you to a pub on the Abingdon-Newbury road (A34) it peters
out there, and you are left on the main road. The proper
Ridgeway Path inclines south-east, over Bury Down.

From East Hendred Down the fine view over the valley is
dominated now by the Atomic Energy Research Establishment at Harwell, a huge complex of buildings which is about
a mile and a half away, but which in some conditions of light
seems so near that you feel you could throw a stone into the
middle of them. The A.E.R.E. is not to be confused with the
Harwell village: it is called Harwell because it is on Harwell
Down, but the village of Harwell, parts of which are still

493896
pretty, lies a mile away to the north-east.

One cannot pretend that atomic energy is attractive. But to
our society, I suppose, it is as necessary for survival as the
Ridgeway forts were to Bronze Age civilization. Whether the
ruins of reactors three thousand years from now will seem as
quiet and remote as the hill-forts I do not know: I doubt it,
and I am unclear whether one will still need a Geiger counter
to go near them even after thousands of years. But time, as
Sir Thomas Browne (1605-82) observed in the seventeenth
century 'hath an art to make a dust of all things'. Perhaps
great monoliths of concrete on Harwell Down will be as
puzzling to our descendants as the Great Stones of Avebury

are to us. It doesn't matter much. The sweep of the Downs here is big enough to absorb atomic energy, and also the enormous cooling towers of Didcot Power Station (actually nearer Sutton Courtenay) three miles or so beyond Harwell. It is a pity that we have to erect such things in a landscape at its best in a sea of cherry blossom (Harwell cherries are famous); but if our industries need atomic energy and our homes electricity, we must site their factories somewhere. On this stretch of the Ridgeway it is perhaps wiser to lift one's eyes to the sky.

But not always; the Thames Valley, for we are nearing the Thames here, has tricks of mist which can make the Atomic Energy Establishment and Didcot Power Station look like fairy palaces. If you walk here on such a day you will not resent these modern concrete edifices, but wonder with excitement at what they can possibly be. There are checks and balances in life, and one must count one's blessings.

The Ridgeway crosses the Abingdon-Newbury road at Gore Hill, and the path then runs almost due south for a mile or so, following the ridge of Several Down to Compton Downs. At least, the Countryside Commission takes the path this way but the Ordnance Survey map continues the old Ridgeway along a footpath running more nearly south-east, making a rather more direct route across the north of Compton Downs to Blewbury Down. There is a network of old paths and trackways here, complicated by the track of an abandoned branch railway line that once ran over the Downs, with some remarkable engineering work in cuttings, from Didcot to Newbury. The various tracks converge at the eastern end of Blewbury Down, and the next mile is a lovely stretch of walking, climbing steadily to the top of Roden Downs and the site (marked on the map) of a Roman Temple, of which nothing at all remains to be seen above ground. Nearby is an older mound or tumulus, both the mound and temple-site bespeaking a long era of sanctity to a succession of the gods whom men once served. It is a quiet, beautiful place, enclosed by a great bend of the Thames, flowing generally west to east between Abingdon and Dorchester, and then north to south

Above Harwell village
Opposite Didcot Power Station from Segsbury ramparts

524825

637823

from Dorchester through Wallingford to Streatley and Goring. From the temple-site the Thames is about eight miles away to the north, but only three and a half miles to the east.

The Thames here is both a geographical and a cultural boundary. In the formative period of the modern English nation it bounded the Saxon kingdom of Wessex and was held as a frontier by Alfred and his sons against the onslaught

of the Danish Vikings. The survival of Wessex south and west of the Thames determined the course of history, ensuring the survival of the English people, and the expansion of English power to rule England. Later, when the Norman William, himself of Viking stock, successfully invaded England, the English were too well established for a new wave of settlers to dispossess them. There was change at the top, but there was no great change of population. A Norman aristocracy was rewarded with English land, but their immediate interest was to hold England against any further attacks from the Continent. After the Battle of Hastings there was no more fighting south and west of the Thames. Harold Godwinson, who had seized the English crown on the death of Edward

the Confessor, and who was killed at Hastings, was regarded by many of the English as a usurper, and they were ready enough to accept William. He was at least related to the old dynasty of Wessex through his great-aunt Emma, who was the mother of Edward the Confessor. One great Saxon thane, Wigod of Wallingford, materially helped William by giving him an uncontested passage of the Thames, and his daughter married one of William's knights.

William's line of castles along the river — London, Windsor, Wallingford, Oxford — secured a base in Southern England from which to subdue the Midlands and the North. Norman soldiers married English women, and within a couple of generations there was a stable Anglo-Norman society — the English absorbed the Normans.

Earlier in history, what was left of Roman-British civilization was preserved by the Thames frontier and the line of Ridgeway forts for at least a generation after the battle of Badon, enabling the misty kingdom of Arthur to grow into legend as a kind of Golden Age.

And earlier still? If it is right to deem the Great Stone Culture of the Bronze Age a civilization, this was its frontier. You can survey it well from the temple-site above the river: behind you the protecting rim of Downs along which you have come from the metropolitan centre of Avebury, and in front the marches of the Thames, which served as a safety belt of no-man's-land between that prehistoric civilization and its less ordered and more primitive neighbours.

The last of the Ridgeway forts is some two miles to the north of the temple-site, not here actually on the Ridgeway, but still protecting it from the north. It stands on the isolated and commanding Blewburton Hill, which rises steeply from the river valley between Blewbury and Aston Upthorp.

The fort is of fair size, enclosing some seven acres. It has been more excavated than most, and has traces of pits where grain was apparently stored for the garrison. The Romans seem to have had no use for it — or indeed, for any of the other

173

Ridgeway forts, preferring their own lines of communication along their roads. But the Saxons had a cemetery and presumably a settlement there, or nearby.

532868   The parts of Blewbury off the main road from Wantage to Reading (A417) are still attractive, but the motor car has
553863   scarred its peace. The neighbouring villages of Aston Upthorpe
557860   and Aston Tirrold lie a little off the main road and are

enchanting picture postcards come to life. Ethelred I of Wessex is said to have heard mass at Aston Upthorpe before he and his more famous brother Alfred met and defeated the Danes at the Battle of Ashdown.

A diversion to the twin Astons and Blewburton Hill is a pleasant two miles of Downland to the main road, along a track leaving the Ridgeway near the temple-site and running a little east of north. Across the main road a walk of rather less than a mile along a lane takes you to the two Astons — Tirrold first, then Upthorpe — and a footpath from Aston Upthorpe climbs Blewburton Hill (half a mile).

From the temple-site there remains only three and a half miles of Ridgeway to the outskirts of Streatley. True to its nature, the track keeps to the crest of the land, but soon begins to descend, as the Downs fall sharply to the gap in the chalk ridge cut by the Thames between Streatley and Goring (just across the bridge from Streatley). Also true to its nature, this final stretch is all through lovely country, with Ham Wood just to the north and then a glorious open stride across Thurle Down.

540865 (margin)

Streatley Warren (margin)

595858 (margin)

Distances from Scutchamer Knob to Streatley	
Scutchamer Knob to Abingdon-Newbury road (A34)	2¾ miles
A34 to foot of Compton Downs	1½ miles
Compton Downs to site of Roman Temple	2 miles
Site of Roman Temple to Streatley	3½ miles
Total Ridgeway walk without diversions	9¾ miles
Diversion from temple-site to Blewburton Hill via Aston Tirrold and Aston Upthorpe and return	7 miles

9 Logistics

If you are fit, and equipped for sleeping under the stars, you will have no problems in walking the Ridgeway: you can start where you please, keep going as long as you care to, and stop where you like. As long as you remember that you will often be several miles from food and water, and make sure you carry both, you need think of nothing but the enchanting countryside.

For carrying water on day walking I use an army water bottle, the old metal kind covered in khaki felt. I like these bottles better than the newer plastic ones, and I think (though this may be prejudice based on old habit) that they keep the water cooler. They may still be obtainable in some army surplus shops. I also carry a small aluminium cup, and an old pewter pocket flask of whisky. This is not so much to drink as neat whisky (though there are occasions for that) as to flavour the water: a teaspoonful of whisky in a cup of water, just turning it the palest straw-colour, makes water ten times as refreshing. That again may be a subjective view, but the practice is one that I have followed for many years in many parts of the world, and I recommend it as useful.

Binoculars add greatly to the enjoyment of any country walk, and are particularly valuable on the Ridgeway, with its extensive views and long, open distances. But don't be led astray by the idea that a large magnification will help you to see better. There is often mist in the atmosphere, and since the lenses will magnify indiscriminately droplets of water vapour as well as whatever you are trying to look at, very powerful glasses can often cloud rather than assist vision. A magnification 6x is about the most practical compromise for general use on the Ridgeway.

If young children, or the demands of earning a living, make it difficult to find time for a camping tour on the Ridgeway, it can be walked in sections, each offering a marvellous day out. There is no great problem in getting back for the night to London, Reading, Oxford, Bristol, Birmingham or most of the other conurbations in the Midlands and Southern England. That is an important part of the value of the Ridgeway Path; it offers remote and lovely walking that really is accessible.

Some approximate distances by road to the starting point at Overton Hill are: London: 80 miles (128 km); Birmingham: 80 miles (128 km); Bristol: 37 miles (60 km); Oxford: 43 miles (69 km); Reading: 39 miles (63 km).

Fifty years ago you did not need a car for access to the countryside; you might have to walk a few miles more and be prepared to get up early and come home late, but a network of railway branch lines and country bus services would get you to most places in England. An evening's homework with Bradshaw would devise a variety of routes to reach starting places for walking the Ridgeway, with a bonus of experiencing those eccentric little branch lines which once endeared the old Great Western Railway to its users (and often maddened them too). Besides these branch lines winding improbably through meadows glowing with cowslips, there were equally improbable halts and little stations on main lines at which occasional trains actually stopped. Progress has done away with all that: the branch lines are gone, and there is no longer a single station between Didcot and Swindon (though there is talk of re-opening a station once useful to the Ridgeway countryside at Challow, between Wantage and Uffington).

You can still contrive a good Ridgeway walk without a car if you are prepared either to limit your objectives somewhat, to sleep out, or to find somewhere to spend a few nights. An oddity of the Ridgeway countryside, which is also part of its charm, is its extreme remoteness relatively near to large centres of population. Apart from its brief metalled stretch near Chiseldon and the Countryside Commission's diversion round Ogbourne St George, there are only three habitations on nearly forty miles of its entire surviving length — the inn at Foxhill, Ridgeway Farm near Bishopstone and another farm above Wantage. With a car on normal roads it means little to be ten miles from a bed: if there is no room at the inn in one village you can drive on to the next. On foot on the high Downs it is another matter. You must leave the Ridgeway for anything up to five miles to reach a village, and the chances of finding a lodging for the night are not good. Many small country pubs have no accommodation, and those that do have a room or two for travellers may be booked up. Farther west, in Somerset and Devon, you are in bed-and-breakfast country, but not here. There are occasional places offering bed and breakfast, but not many: long-distance tourists will be driving out from hotels at Oxford, Bath or Stratford-on-Avon, day tourists will be going home. If you are not equipped to sleep out, Ridgeway walking must be confined to sections which you can cover and return from in a day, or must be planned carefully in advance.

232813, 253827, 402844

There is a reasonable approach by rail to Avebury and Overton Hill from Pewsey, on the Paddington-Westbury line. A through train does the journey in about an hour and a quarter. From Pewsey you have a walk of about six miles to Overton Hill, the first couple of miles on roads but afterwards through the delectable country climbing to the Wansdyke with magnificent views over the Vale of Pewsey whenever you care to look back. If you can manage twenty miles of fairly rough going in a day, you can go straight on to Foxhill (but if you are planning to spend the night at the Shepherd's Rest make sure that you have booked). This means cutting out exploration round Avebury and the interesting diversion to Fyfield Down, so it may be preferable to arrange to spend the night either at Avebury or Marlborough (four miles from Overton) and go on next day. From Foxhill the next place where you can be reasonably sure of a bed (but again it is wise to book) is Wantage, a Ridgeway walk, without diversions, of some thirteen or fourteen miles. With diversions to the Blowing Stone and the Seven Barrows you should reckon on about

103699, 187692

398880
324872

twenty miles. From Wantage, again without diversions, another fifteen miles will take you to Streatley, where you can get a train to Paddington (the station is Goring-and-Streatley).

806603

For a single day's outing without a car you could start at the Streatley end of the Ridgeway, going by train to Goring-and-Streatley and then walking up to Compton Downs and back (about twelve miles) or, less far, to Roden Downs and the Roman Temple Site and back (roughly eight miles).

806603

Some country buses still exist, and if the planets are in particularly felicitous conjunction for your horoscope you may find a bus to help you. It would be tempting fate to count on it, and even if you come across a bus stop you may find yourself waiting several days for a bus, for some services run only once or twice a week. If you are a passionate and determined bus-addict, you can still make use of buses, but time-tables and services change, and you should inquire about up-to-date information on bus routes in the area.

If you get stuck somewhere, finding youself more tired than you expected, make for the nearest village and telephone Swindon, Wantage or Marlborough for a taxi. As country bus services have diminished taxi services have grown, and longish journeys to remote villages are accepted as a matter of course.

1584, 398880, 187692

The most practicable access to the Ridgeway for most people nowadays will be by car. If you have your own transport you can please yourself, but if you are driving yourself you must double any distance you propose to walk because you must walk back to where you have left the car. There is, therefore, much to be said for planning a series of Ridgeway walks with someone who is prepared to drive while you walk: in families with young children one parent with an older child may do the walking, the other the driving; and they can alternate from day to day. From London the M4 motorway — whose engineers merit high praise for the unobtrusive way in which they have sculpted this great road through the Downs — is probably the best approach. Leaving the motor-

360727

179

way at Junction 14 for Hungerford and the A4, another
187692   twelve miles or so will bring you to Marlborough, with many
103699   inns and eating places. Marlborough to Overton Hill is four
miles, to Avebury another mile and a half.

If the walking party starts along the Ridgeway at Overton
Hill the next convenient access by car is five and a half miles
on at Barbury Castle, reached by a metalled minor road from
146805   Wroughton (two and a half miles). There is good access by
207800   road at the foot of Liddington Castle (four miles' walk from
Barbury) and, if you take the Countryside Commission's
203742   route, in the village of Ogbourne St George (also about four
miles on from Barbury by Smeathe's Ridge).

To translate Ridgeway distances into time you should reckon
about two and a half miles to the hour. Tigers can do more,
of course, and so can ordinary mortals, if driven, but you are
not making a forced march, and this is a reasonable speed
over fairly rough going. That makes Overton Hill to Barbury
Castle a little over two hours (without diversions) and Overton Hill to Liddington or Ogbourne St George a trifle under
four hours of actual walking time. Then you must allow time
for rest and reflection. Ten minutes in the hour is a good
working rule for rest periods over a long walk, but that is for
physical rest, not for the leisurely enjoyment of a meal, or
for the sheer luxury of lying back and letting oneself be
absorbed by the sky. Walking for pleasure with a meal and a
drink on the way, I should allow three hours from Overton
to Barbury, and about five hours from Overton to Liddington
and Ogbourne St George.

For the car-party an excursion into Savernake Forest would
be a good way of spending three to five hours. Savernake is,
to my thinking, the most beautiful woodland in England, and
its Grand Avenue — four miles between colonnades of great
trees — is scarcely matched anywhere in the world. The forest
is easily reached from the main road, A4, which runs through
its outskirts on approaching Marlborough from the east.
210684   Leave the main road at a place marked Forest Hill, where two
roads branch off into the forest proper, one running south-

west and the other, which is the Grand Avenue, south-east. A drive to Savernake, and an hour or so under its great beeches would allow comfortable time for getting to Barbury or Liddington to pick up the walkers. And the car-party is not to be assumed permanently car-borne: if the car gets to Barbury or Liddington before the walkers, there are great hill-forts to be explored and the serene view to be enjoyed.

If you intend going back to London after the rendezvous at
192808 Barbury or Liddington, you can rejoin the M4 at Junction 15,
just a mile north of Chiseldon. If you have met at Ogbourne
203742 St George you can have a lovely drive through Ramsbury and
along the north bank of the River Kennett to get back to the
360727 motorway at Junction 14. This is not the way you came to
Marlborough: the route by Hungerford and the A4 takes you
south of the Kennet; the Ramsbury route is north of the river.
If you are not planning to go home, a car puts you within
1584, 288956, 215996 reach of Swindon, Faringdon, Lechlade and a number of
other places where you can find hotels or residential inns.

For the next walk, the following day, or on the next outing, you can rejoin the Ridgeway where you left it, and you have more frequent access places than on the Marlborough Downs. Between Foxhill and Wantage, good access places are:

253827 The crossing by Ridgeway Farm south of Bishopstone
273843 The B4000 crossing south-east of Ashbury
295859 By Woolstone Hill to the Ridgeway just under a mile east of Wayland's Smithy
297866 By Dragon Hill to the foot of Uffington Castle, where there is a car park
323864 On Blowingstone Hill
344851 At the top of Sparsholt Hill, junction with B4001
372841 By Gramp's Hill, south of Letcombe Bassett
394844 At the crossing of A338, the Wantage-Hungerford road
417842 At the crossing of B4494, the Wantage-Newbury road

While the walking party makes its way between Foxhill and
Wantage, the car-party has a choice of many attractive little
towns, depending on the rendezvous and time available. The
201924 road through Ashbury (B4000) runs north-west to Highworth

(five and a half miles) and from there it is only another five
miles on the A351 to the beautiful old town of Lechlade and
215996
the upper reaches of the Thames. East of Lechlade (two and a
half miles) by lanes from the B4449 is William Morris's
252989
dream-like village of Kelmscot, with the old manor house
where he lived. The house is open to visitors, but not every
day. It belongs to the Society of Antiquaries, and the details
of dates on which it is open may be obtained from the Society
at Burlington House, Piccadilly, London. Then there are the
294877, 283871
entrancing villages of Woolstone and Compton Beauchamp at
the foot of Whitehorse Hill itself, recommended as a diversion
in Chapter 6. The car-party should make sure of visiting
281854, 298864
Wayland's Smithy and Uffington Castle, to both of which
there is easy access by road. If you are staying in the district,
Wantage is a convenient place to spend the night.

Another good excursion, easily made from Wantage (via
Faringdon on the A417 and then the Swindon road A420,
roughly ten miles) or from Lechlade (main road A417 toward
Buscot, then taking a minor road through the valley of the
Rover Cole to Coleshill, roughly six miles) is to Great Coxwell
268942
and the most magnificent barn in England. William Morris
described it as 'noble as a cathedral', and it is indeed built like
a cathedral, with a great arching nave and aisles. It was built
in the thirteenth century, and although often called a 'tithe
barn' it is not, but it is, in fact, more interesting. It was built
for the monks of Beaulieu Abbey to house the produce from
their own considerable estates round Faringdon (given to
Beaulieu Abbey by King John). The size of the barn gives one
a sudden insight into the enormous wealth of the great
religious houses of the Middle Ages.

Between Wantage and the Thames at Streatley there are also
several access places to the Ridgeway, but if the walking
party is going on to Streatley an intermediate rendezvous
may not be needed. It may be helpful, however, to make the
diversion to Aston Upthorpe and Blewburton Hill by car, and
a good meeting place for this is at the end of the Downs Road
from Blewbury (A417) by Churn Hill. If the car-party has the
best part of a day to fill in while waiting for the walkers to get

4997

506972

to Streatley, the time can be spent pleasantly in Abingdon (nine miles from Wantage). There is a beautiful short walk along the Thames from Abingdon Bridge to Abingdon Lock, and there are boats to be hired for enjoying the river itself. From Abingdon to Streatley by road is about fifteen miles (A34 to Rowstock, near Harwell, and then A417 to Streatley).

For all its remoteness on foot, car-distances in the Ridgeway countryside are not great, and given car-transport for access to the walking route the logistical problems are slight. But all expeditions require planning, and in a car-borne age it is sometimes hard to appreciate that once you have left the car you may have to walk five miles to buy a box of matches. Do not underestimate the Ridgeway: it is in the gentle English countryside with no physical dangers from wild animals, but once you have set foot upon it you are on your own. It is good for the spirit that it should be so; it is a very real part of the refreshment of a Ridgeway walk, but it may need a little mental adjustment. The need to carry food and water is readily acceptable: you do that for any picnic. Less easy to accept is the extreme difficulty, almost the impossibility, of finding a casual lodging for the night unless you can get to a town. The towns I have mentioned possess hotels, but they are not thick with hotels and bed-and-breakfast places, so it is wise to use the AA or RAC book or some other hotel guide, and telephone beforehand to make sure that you have a place to go. Of course you may have friends in the locality, or live near enough to get home from a Ridgeway walk, but even so you must secure your transport and make sure that you can walk the distance you have planned to meet it: there are no passing cars to give a lift on the Ridgeway.

As in most circumstances in life, it is best to be self-contained and independent. That means travelling equipped to camp out, which also means carrying the equipment. That notable walker John Hillaby carried a pack weighing thirty-five pounds (including a tent) on his walk from Land's End to John O'Groats.* This is not a savage weight, but it is enough, and it can soon seem formidable if you are not used to being

*John Hillaby, *Journey Through Britain* (Constable, London, 1968).

so burdened. Hillaby trained himself by carrying a rucksack loaded with weight-lifter's weights on walks through London. Water is an additional problem on the Ridgeway, for if you plan to camp out a single water bottle is not enough. If you are going to be self-sufficient for twenty-four hours you will need at least a gallon of water for drinking, cooking, and such washing as you may do, and that alone weighs ten pounds. You can manage on less, but not with comfort. Your weight of water will reduce as you use it, and if you don't want to start off with as much as a gallon you can descend for water at intervals, but that means adding several miles to your walk.

It is easier if there are two people to share the load, but this calls for twice as much food and water, a double tent or two one-man tents, two sleeping bags, etc. You can save a bit of weight because you don't need two sets of cooking equipment, but the net saving is not much. For two or three nights on the Ridgeway you will not need to carry much in the way of spare clothing, but it is folly not to take some: after a long day's walking socks at least are better changed, and there is much comfort in being able to change a sweat-soaked shirt. If you are an experienced mountaineer or rock-climber you will have your own methods for dealing with all this, and your own schemes for keeping down weight. But it is not quite enough to be an experienced *camper*, for much camping nowadays is done by car, and tents and cooking equipment that are no problem when carried by car may ruin a walk if you try to carry them on your back. If you are not already equipped for *walking camping* go to a specialist mountaineering shop and take advice. A Ridgeway walk is not mountaineering, but mountain climbers have developed some marvellously lightweight equipment, and the less weight you have on your back the more you will enjoy your walk. There is, I think, an ideal solution to this problem — a donkey. The donkey carries the load and you carry the compass and the map. For centuries pack-animals did most of the inland transport in Britain: they can go where carts cannot, and for most of the Ridgeway's history they were as familiar as men on its rough path. When I planned this book I intended to see if I could travel with a donkey — 'Travels with a Donkey on the Ridgeway' might, I hoped, earn a modest place in the shadow of Robert Louis Stevenson's famous *Travels with a Donkey in the Cevennes*. Two things prevented me from carrying out my plan. First I was ill for two months, which upset my timetable, and then I had reluctantly to accept that twentieth-century England offered far fewer facilities for donkeys than had nineteenth-century France. To get the donkey to the Ridgeway I either needed some form of horse-box or faced miles of trudging with the donkey on main roads. There was the further difficulty that I had no donkey, and no practicable means of keeping one if I had. But I still think that a donkey with panniers would be a good friend on a Ridgeway walk, companionable but not talkative, and very useful indeed.

For those who ride, the Ridgeway runs through magnificent horse country, but remember that although the track is a right of way most of the land is privately owned, and if you are planning a riding trek you should make sure beforehand where you may ride and where you may not. The inviting gallops that you see are maintained by training stables, and unauthorized riders may get into trouble. On foot or on horseback you should also watch out for rabbit holes, for a rabbit hole may all too easily sprain a human ankle, or break a horse's leg.

On foot, donkeyless, and shouldering your own pack, a little fatigue towards the end of a day does not greatly matter. It is the lot of man, and you tread where countless generations have trodden. And by carrying your pack you have earned that rewarding moment when you slip it from your shoulders and lean against a bank, or a nicely hollowed sarsen, to gaze into the sky. You cannot have it otherwise; such moments must be earned and the reward is infinite. You have walked timelessly for a little, made yourself one with the tillers of those brave small fields scratched with sticks out of the hill-side, one with the movers of the Great Stones, one with the pilgrims, pedlars and soldiers who have walked here, and walked on.

10 Birds, Beasts and Flowers

In 1966 I led a small expedition in an elderly sailing boat across the North Atlantic, via Iceland and Greenland, to try to work out the route by which the Viking Leif Eiriksson discovered America some five centuries before Columbus got there. Feeling that we should be sailing in regions where there would be many interesting sea birds, we equipped ourselves with various bird-books. Alas, they were all too expert: we were instructed to study the colour and shape of a bird's feet, but the birds we met were either flying or swimming, and we never saw their feet. So there was nothing for it but simply to enjoy watching the birds, the little ones we knew, like Mother Carey's chickens, and the many beautiful ones that had to remain nameless. We added nothing to ornithology, but we did enjoy the birds, particularly when we were endangered by ice, when the nonchalance of the birds sitting on icebergs was curiously comforting.

By naming things, man has always given himself an imagined power over them: this is a very old human characteristic, the source of much of the power and prestige of priests, doctors and wise men. I ought to be able to tell readers of this book the name of every little furry creature that scuttles across the Ridgeway Path, of every tiny wild flower that glows like a jewel in the setting of the downland turf. I cannot. I can but try to share my rudimentary North Atlantic technique of simply enjoying wild life.

At various times in the very distant past the Ridgeway countryside supported lions, bison, mammoths, reindeer, wolves and numerous other wild animals. All these are long departed. The wolf and the wild cat lasted into historical times — the hamlet of Catmore, three miles south of Scutch-hamer Knob on the Ridgeway, gets its name from a wild cat that once lived by a pond or mere there. But wolf and wild cat alike disappeared many centuries ago. As fierce and brave as the wild cat, but less dangerous to man because of the difference in our relative sizes (to which these little wild creatures owe their survival in England) are the stoat and the weasel. You may see one or the other running fast and low to cross the path in front of you. They look much alike, but the weasel is smaller, and more reddish in colour, and the stoat has a black tab at the end of his tail. Neither will trouble you, but if you wish to pursue acquaintance, the weasel is said to have a nicer character than the stoat.

In spite of myxomatosis, there are still plenty of rabbits on the Downs, inhabiting the warrens (sometimes marked as such on the map) where they have congregated since being brought to England (supposedly) by the Romans. Rabbits are entrancing little creatures to watch, but it is as well that there are foxes, stoats — and man himself — to keep them down, for they compete with man and his farm animals for food, and their holes can be dangerous to human and horse legs.

There are doubtless some adders on the Downs, though I have never seen one, and, like most snakes, they are anxious to keep out of man's way. Unless trodden on or deliberately vexed, they are unlikely to harm you.

I can, and do, spend hours watching birds, but can name only a few. The best of the Ridgeway birds for me is the skylark, with its marvellous vertical take-off, and magical, hovering song. Hawks are beautiful, though there is always a sort of grimness in their beauty. On the rim of the Devil's Punchbowl, and at other places where the escarpment falls steeply, you can sometimes enjoy the rare experience of being *above* a hovering hawk, and looking down on the upper surface of his wings. There is much other bird-life around the Ridgeway, and the birds — even if you are as ignorant as I am — are among the joys of a Ridgeway walk.

I am slightly better on flora than on fauna, because my childhood Sunday reading was often the Rev. C.A. Johns's *Flowers of the Field*. My edition was published in 1881, and that edition is the eighteenth, but it is still, I think, one of the best books on English wild flowers ever written. It is stiff reading for a child, but the names of the flowers fascinated me, and the illustrations are superb. There are some rare lichens to be found on some of the sarsens around Avebury, but you have to be an expert to identify them. If you are exceptionally lucky you may come across the rare (and rarely beautiful) *Anemone Pulsatilla*, or 'Pasque Flower', but if you do, don't disclose where you have seen it, for as a wild flower (though it can be grown in gardens) it is dangerously near extinction. The Pasque Flower blooms in April or May, and it is an exquisite violet-blue colour.

The *Primulaceae*, or primrose tribe, are richly spread in the Ridgeway countryside, and are a particular delight. The cowslip is becoming rare as more and more of England gets built up, but it is still quite common on banks and hollows of the Downs. The miniature cowslips that manage to survive on the exposed heights around the Devil's Punchbowl are exceptionally interesting and very pretty. Also lovely is the 'Poor Man's Weather-Glass' *(Anagallis arvensis)*, perhaps more commonly known as the Scarlet Pimpernel. It is an unobtrusive but charming little plant, which gets its country name from its habit of shutting up its scarlet petals when it is going to rain. Don't be disturbed, though, if you meet it with its petals shut in the afternoon, for either it expects the worst of the English climate and assumes rain every afternoon, or it just likes going to sleep, for it seldom opens its petals in the afternoon anyway. In the morning it is quite a good guide to the weather, so don't plan a picnic if you see it with its petals shut well before noon.

But flowers are not put into the world to be read about. The best guide to the wild flowers of the Ridgeway is to go and look at them. Whether you know their Latin, or even their English, names or not, they give a lift to the spirit on the dullest day.

11 The Continuation of the Ridgeway

The road that is still the ancient Ridgeway ends where it meets the Thames. From the Wansdyke on the Pewsey escarpment to Streatley on the Thames, the track runs now as it was trodden in remote prehistory. Apart from the diversion round Ogbourne St George, the Countryside Commission's modern signposts from Overton Hill to Streatley point the way along the oldest road in Britain, perhaps in Europe, still in continuous use. Across the Thames the scene changes.

The Countryside Commission's signposted walk called the Ridgeway Path goes on into the Chilterns, and it is still delightful walking country. But it is a different countryside. The high bare Downs have changed to the lower, wooded Chiltern Hills, a place of parks and country houses, ringed by small towns. Nearer to London and more thickly populated, the modern Chiltern countryside has no room for a wide and unenclosed Ridgeway. The Commission's extension of its Ridgeway Path is a skilfully contrived network of footpaths and medieval rights of way.

In antiquity, the Thames was both more of a barrier and more of a highway than it is now. It was a barrier to tribal settlement and the jurisdiction of local chieftains just as it formed a county boundary for almost its entire length until the local government reorganization of 1974. But the river was also a highway, a route to the heart of England for invaders with boats from north-west Germany and Scandinavia, and an internal trade route throughout prehistory and history until the coming of railways in the last century. Early man used the

Thames and often stopped at the Thames, making his habitations on its gravel terraces, and looking to the river for protection on his flank. But man is also a wanderer, and not all our ancient forbears were content with settled lives. Merchants in antiquity, as now, sought international trade, and they and their salesmen travelled between tribal settlements. Thus places where the river could be forded by human porters or by pack-animals (oxen before horses) were of great importance. There was such a ford where Streatley now is, and its particular value in antiquity was that once across the river you could climb almost at once to the chalk escarpment of the Chilterns and find an upland route similar to the Ridgeway to continue travelling north-east. The Goring Gap here in the chalk ridge across Southern England, cut by the Thames some millions of years ago, is little wider than the river and its immediate flood plain, and it could be crossed quickly to regain the relative safety of high ground.

Precisely where the ford was is unclear, but tradition has it that it was more or less on the line of the present Streatley-Goring bridge, and tradition is probably right. There was no bridge until 1838, when a wooden bridge was built to replace a ferry that had plied for centuries; from medieval times the ferry rights belonged to Goring Priory, passing into private hands when the Priory was suppressed by Henry VIII. Between the ferry points the river was often fairly shallow and it is said that in the eighteenth century adventurous young bloods would occasionally drive a coach across the river bed. The crossing, however, must often have been perilous: in 1674 a party of revellers returning to Streatley from Goring Feast upset the ferry boat and no fewer than sixty of them are reported to have been drowned.* (It seems a large number, but perhaps there was more than one boat.) The wooden bridge of 1838 was replaced by a concrete bridge in 1920.

There was a better crossing — also used in antiquity and

*Sad and Deplorable News from Oxfordsheir & Barksheir, printed at The Little Old Baily (1674). Quoted by F.S. Thacker in The Thames Highway, Vol.II (David and Charles, Devon, 1968).

certainly preferred by the Romans, who had a fortified post there — five miles upstream at Wallingford. Some of the early Ridgeway travellers may equally have preferred this crossing, for it could be reached readily enough from the Downs by descending a little north of the track to Streatley.

To what extent there was much through traffic beyond the Thames in very ancient times is impossible to say; there was some, for the flint mines at Grimes Graves in Norfolk had an export trade over much of England and the Beaker merchants would not have neglected this prosperous centre of pre-historic industry. Later, there was considerably more coming and going, and the lower road, the Icknield Way, which we have already met near Wantage, had a recognized continuation across the Thames, via the Chilterns and Bedfordshire to East Anglia. It is the Icknield Way, or rather the general line of it, for much of the old route has been embodied in modern roads, that the Ridgeway Path follows from Goring to Ivinghoe Beacon, some four miles north-east of Tring.

The map still shows stretches of road called Icknield Way, but they are marked under two names, Upper Icknield Way and Lower Icknield Way. As with the Ridgeway and the Icknield Way near Wantage, the two routes run roughly para-llel, the road along the lower contour serving the villages along the spring-line. Probably the Upper Icknield Way is more nearly the continuation of the ancient Ridgeway, the lower road having taken its name as travellers took to it.

There are fewer logistical problems about a walking tour in the Chilterns than in the Ridgeway Downs. There is easier access both by train and by Green Line bus from London and as the area is more populous there are more useful local bus services. In addition to the railway station at Goring, you can get by train to Prince's Risborough, Wendover and Tring, all of which give near access to various stretches of the Country-side Commission's Path. For access by road you have a large choice of rendezvous with a car, for the walking route runs much nearer to modern roads here than on the Ridgeway side of the Thames. And if you need a lodging for the night there

are many more places where you can look for accommodation.

The whole route of the Countryside Commission's continuation of its Ridgeway Path through the Chilterns offers some forty miles of grand walking from the Thames at Goring to
959168 Ivinghoe Beacon, only half a dozen miles from Dunstable. Making an early start from Goring, you can cover the route comfortably in three days, with two nights sleeping out — or you have a fair choice of accessible inns and hotels along the way, at Stokenchurch, Prince's Risborough, Wendover and Tring. Being more accessible than the older Ridgeway across the Thames, the Chiltern Path is admirably suited for day walking. Goring to Nuffield provides one pleasant stretch of about eight miles, starting off along the Thames to Monge-
611882 well Park, about a mile north of the village of North Stoke, then turning east to follow the line of an interesting old earthwork (marked on the map as yet another Grim's Ditch) to
667874 Nuffield. At Nuffield you have good road access to the main road to Maidenhead, A423, with access there to the M4
8002 motorway. From Nuffield to Prince's Risborough is a stretch of some fourteen to fifteen miles, with convenient breaks at

689945, 757010   Watlington (five miles) and Chinnor (five and a half miles on from Watlington and two and a half miles from Prince's Risborough).

8002, 869078   Prince's Risborough to Wendover is not much more than five miles in distance, but it may well be covered slowly, for the route runs through some of the loveliest country in the

843057   Chilterns, skirting Chequers, the country house of prime ministers in office, and reaching Wendover over the magnifi-

869078   cent escarpment of Coombe Hill, with wonderful views across the Vale of Aylesbury.

869078, 952123   Wendover to Tring Station — by the path, which is not very direct — is about seven miles, and Tring Station to Ivinghoe

959168   Beacon another three miles: a day's walk of ten miles, or two comfortable stretches, the final stretch to Ivinghoe Beacon being again through particularly beautiful high country.

In his book called *The Icknield Way* Anthony Bulfield traces the old road from Hunstanton on the Norfolk coast of the

Wash via Thetford, Newmarket, Royston, Hitchin, Luton, Dunstable, Tring and Wendover to Goring. Across the Thames he traces the old road along the modern Streatley-Wantage road (A417), out of Wantage on the Swindon road (B4507), through Bishopstone and Wanborough where, in his view, the old route went off south-west through Chiseldon to join the Ridgeway at Liddington Castle. I am sure that he is right as far as Wanborough, but I am less certain about his junction with the Ridgeway for the last few miles to or from Avebury. By the time the Icknield Way came into use the other route over the high Downs served different needs: it was a track for shepherds and their flocks, and it may also have retained a military use as a direct link between the great hill-forts. Ordinary travellers and traders with pack-animals turned to the lower route because it gave easier access to water, and because their journeys were concerned with the settlements that grew up on the spring-line and below it.

Therefore it seems to me more probable that the low road to and from Avebury did not go into the high Downs but more or less followed the track of the modern Avebury-Swindon road (A361) to Wroughton, branching east there to go through Chiseldon and Liddington village (a mile north of the fort) to join the known track of the Icknield Way to the Thames at Wanborough. But the Icknield Way, serving villages and settlements that have grown into towns, has been so much absorbed into later road systems that, except where the old name has survived locally, one can only guess precisely where it went.

Ridgeway — Icknield Way — Ridgeway Path . . . The road runs through time as well as space and the wayfarer walks history. Governments do so many things to restrict freedom that it is good to have an arm of government reaching out to secure the ancient freedom of the footpath. The Countryside Commission's establishment of a right of way by foot from Avebury to Ivinghoe offers a wonderful journey through a landscape patterned by the feet of every generation from the Old Stone Age, and fashioned by digging-stick, plough and tractor to make England.

تمام شد

Further Reading

My mother's people have lived in the White Horse country-side for near a thousand years and it is still my home. When you write about your home it is, alas, impossible to recall the source of every fact and fable that has gone into it, and if unwittingly I have drawn on anyone's work without acknow-ledgment I can but ask forgiveness. I have drawn, inevitably, on research I did for my own regional study, *The Upper Thames* (Eyre and Spottiswoode, London, 1970, revised edition Eyre Methuen, London, 1974), the sources of which were all acknowledged there.

Topography covers a multitude of academic fields, and the ideal topographical writer should be the ideal polymath. Short of this (a long way short for most of us) one can only read as widely as possible. Considering the Ridgeway country-side under the following general headings, books that I have found particularly helpful, and which I warmly recommend for further reading, include:

Archaeology and Pre-History

R.J.C. Atkinson, *Stonehenge and Avebury* (H.M. Stationery Office, London, 1959; revised edition 1971)
D. Emerson Chapman, *Is This Your First Visit to Avebury?* (H.M. Stationery Office, London, 1947).
Glyn Daniel, *The Megalith Builders of Western Europe*, (Hutchinson, London, 1958; new edition, Penguin, Harmondsworth, 1962) and
P.J. Fowler, *Wessex*, 'Regional Archaeologies' (Heinemann Educational Books, London, 1967) and papers in *Current Archaeology*.
Jacquetta Hawkes, *A Guide to the Prehistoric and Roman Monuments in England and Wales* (Chatto and Windus, London, 1951; revised 1973)
Stuart Piggott, *West Kennett Long Barrow* (H.M. Stationery Office, London, 1971)

Then there are the invaluable specialist maps published by the Ordnance Survey: 'Southern Britain in the Iron Age' (covering the period roughly from the beginning of the fifth century B.C. to the middle of the first century A.D.); 'Roman Britain' (A.D. 43 to 410); 'Britain in the Dark Ages' (A.D. 410 to 870). The two latter extend, of course, into the historical period, but include much important archaeological information.

History

Geoffrey Ashe (ed.), *The Quest for Arthur's Britain* (Pall Mall, London, 1968).

Bede, *A History of the English Church and People* (the edition I use is the excellent translation by Leo Sherley-Price, Penguin, Harmondsworth, 1955)

Keith Feiling, *A History of England* (Macmillan, London, 1950)

John Morris, *The Age of Arthur* (Weidenfield and Nicolson, London, 1973)

I.A. Richmond, *Roman Britain* (Penguin, Harmondsworth, 1955)

Dorothy Whitelock, *The Beginnings of English Society* (Penguin, Harmondsworth, 1952; revised edition, 1965)

David Wilson, *The Anglo-Saxons* (Thames and Hudson, London 1960; Penguin revised edition, Harmondsworth, 1971)

Geology and Landscape

W.G. Hoskins, *The Making of the English Landscape* (Hodder and Stoughton, London, 1958)

L. Dudley Stamp, *Britain's Structure and Scenery* (Collins, London, 1966)

Architecture and General Topography

R.P. Beckinsale, *Companion into Berkshire* (Methuen, London, 1951; new edition Spurbooks, Bourne End, 1972)

F.G. Brabant, *Berkshire* (Methuen, London, 1911; revised edition 1934)

Anthony Bulfield, *The Icknield Way* (Terence Dalton, Lavenham, 1972)

Richard Jefferies, *Wild Life in a Southern County* (Smith, Elder, London, 1879), *Bevis, The Story of a Boy* (Jonathan Cape, London, 1932), *The Story of My Heart* (new edition Macmillan, London, 1968)

Arthur Mee, *Wiltshire* (Hodder and Stoughton, London, 1939)

Sir Nikolaus Pevsner, *Berkshire* (Penguin, Harmondsworth, 1966), and *Wiltshire* (new edition, Penguin, Harmondsworth, 1975)

Pamela Street, *Portrait of Wiltshire* (Robert Hale, London, 1971)

H.W. Timperley, *Ridge Way Country* (Dent, London, 1935)

Place-Names

Kenneth Cameron, *English Place Names* (Batsford, London, 1961)

Eilert Ekwall, *The Oxford Dictionary of English Place-Names* (Oxford University Press, London, 1936; 4th edition 1960)

Birds, Beasts and Flowers

S. Vere Benson, *Birds* (Observer's pocket series, Frederick Warne, London, 1960)

H.J.M. Bowen, *The Flora of Berkshire* (Holywell Press, Oxford, 1968)

C.A. Johns, *Flowers of the Field*, 18th edition (Society for Promoting Christian Knowledge, London, 1881)

Observer's books of British wild life

W.J. Stokoe, *Butterflies* (Observer's pocket series, Frederick Warne, London, 1937)

Index

198